"This book is the perfect companion for someone who is early in the process of psychotherapy. It is ideal for therapists to give to clients. It illustrates through several case examples many important concepts such as the sensory and logical brain, the function of emotions, and the importance of a support system. The awareness exercises are very useful."

—Richard G. Erskine, Ph.D.
international trainer of Integrative Psychotherapy

"What a revelation! The Power of Connection walks the reader through how to do the wonderful work Dr. Bea does in person, helping people to process their emotions so that they can do it even if they are not with Bea. Freedom awaits. I will be sharing this book with all of my clients. It is well laid out, and the illustrations add depth and beauty. A wonderful book that I will keep close as a constant reminder."

—Emma Holmes, coach

"Thanks to the clear and concise information laid out in the book, I'm sure many people will be helped with their troubling emotions in these pandemic times. By including case studies and interesting illustrations, Bea Mackay has made her points very understandable. She has written a very helpful and much-needed book for our time."

—Norma Berkey, retired teacher

"The Power of Connection is an elegantly written and beautifully illustrated book that is both engaging and accessible. It is an owner's manual to help the reader better understand the mysterious and essential part of our being that is our emotional life. The complexity of how brain structure, brain health, and emotional management fit together is explained in clear and concise terms and is supported by many real-life clinical examples that are easy to relate to. This book explains what it actually means to work through our emotions in therapy and how building emotional vocabulary enhances our ability to communicate and deepen relationships with others. It also offers hope that even long-held self-defeating beliefs and behaviours can change over time through experiencing empathy, understanding, and acceptance towards self and others."

—Lindsay Stewart, social worker

"This book is essential for therapists and psychologists to recommend to all their clients. It presents current thinking and research on brain science linked to a practical approach to supporting people with lots of techniques to change their lives. It is brought alive by beautiful graphics and is full of exercises and client stories along with a profoundly simple summary at the end of each chapter about how to live from what has been discussed. Highly recommended, and awareness is the key!"

—Brian O'Neill, psychologist and Gestalt therapist

"The Power of Connection could also be called a user's guide to the human experience. In clear, jargon-free language, Bea Mackay has captured what it means to be fully present and to participate in this thing we call life. Bea shows us the difference between managing our lives and experiencing our lives in ways that are satisfying and at the same time productive. In The Power of Connection, we learn how to tap into the gifts we are given from birth, and the reader quickly learns the difference between managing emotion and processing emotion. These two very different realms of experience are both necessary for living a full life. Bea guides us through sorting out sensations, identifying and accessing emotions, and moving towards acceptance of what is. Or, in her words, "What is, is." Her antidote comes to us in the form of a book chock-full of tips, examples, and suggestions for building a more contactful life and raising healthier, happier children. Your family won't regret you reading this book, and they very well may pick it up when you are finished!"

—Charlie Bowman, president of the Indianapolis Gestalt Institute

"Dr. Bea Mackay has provided the reader with excellent strategies to develop and enhance self-understanding and connection with self and others. Her lucid explanations of neuroscience and mindful self-grounding using the breath as an anchor enable the reader to understand how one can integrate feelings and emotions by processing them without getting lost in them by trying to over-manage and control them. Dr. Mackay clarifies how our universal capacity for processing and integration creates deeper connections and creative new enriching patterns of living."

—Susan Burak, B.A., J.D., M.A., R.C.C., lawyer,
certified mediator, and registered clinical counsellor

The POWER *of* CONNECTION

How to process emotion in turbulent times.

By Bea Mackay, Ph. D.

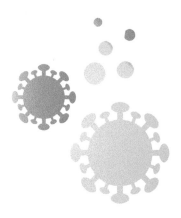

◆ FriesenPress

One Printers Way
Altona, MB R0G 0B0
Canada

www.friesenpress.com

Written by Bea Mackay
Edited by Tereza Racekova
Graphics by Lesley Wexler
Coordinated by Bree BV

beainbalance.com

ISBN
 978-1-5255-9758-9 (Hardcover)
978-1-5255-9757-2 (Paperback)
978-1-5255-9759-6 (eBook)

1. Self-Help, Emotions

Distributed to the trade by The Ingram Book Company

To ALEXIS
HAPPY READING!

B.

To all the frontline workers
in the fight against COVID-19

BEA MACKAY PH.D

breathe through
the sensations

Contents

Acknowledgements

I want to thank my publishing team, who I am incredibly proud of and who made this book possible. We worked so well together, each providing our expertise. It was so much fun!

I want to thank Tereza Racekova, my amazing editor, who took my material and made it flow like magic.

I want to thank Lesley Wexler, my incredible graphic artist, who created the brilliant cover, images, diagrams, and pictures for this book.

I want to thank Bree BV, my remote assistant, who effectively organized our project. She brought our team together in a fun and efficient way. She's a super organizer, extremely patient, and helpful.

Lastly, I want to thank Maurice Basset, who suggested that I take my book, *Let Things Fall Together*, and create a shorter version of it. Without his idea, this book would not have come to fruition.

Preface

"In the beginning there was . . ." —The Bible

As I write this, the world is in turmoil about the coronavirus pandemic. I am in Montreal on a writing retreat, working with my editor, Tereza. I am scheduled to fly home to Vancouver tomorrow morning—at least I hope I am.

However, things could change at any second.

Tereza is not feeling well today. I'm hoping she is just tired or has a cold and not the virus. My flight to Vancouver could be cancelled, or the airports in Montreal and Vancouver could be closed. There is constant

PANDEMIC

news of shutting things down, including large events, conferences, the NBA basketball season, major tennis tournaments (basically, any gatherings over 500 people), and flights from most of Europe to the USA. News of the latest breakouts of the virus is being announced on an ongoing basis.

I never have in all my years experienced a global pandemic. People all over the world are frightened to various degrees.

A pandemic (of a disease) means it is prevalent throughout an entire country, continent, or the world. However, it is also used to describe an emotion, such as fear, which can be widespread globally. Because of technology, most news is rapidly spreading across countries and continents.

The word "panic" is embedded in the word "pandemic." How we, the citizens of the world, handle a pandemic is a crucial factor. The real issue of a deadly virus that is spreading rapidly and needs to be controlled quickly is one thing—a concrete concern to be fearful of and promptly acted upon in effective ways.

However, the fear people have about the spread of the virus is another pandemic that needs to be contained. People need to be supported, encouraged, and forced to focus on preventing the spread of the virus. This type of pandemic is not concrete. Therefore, it is more difficult to control.

When people get frightened, they go into the Fight, Flight, Freeze modes. Specifically, they go into survival mode. When something like a pandemic occurs, people naturally scurry to build up a supply of necessary items, such as water, food, prescribed and over-the-counter medications, medical supplies, and appropriate clothing. This is sensible and wise behaviour.

However, this sensible behaviour may escalate into irrational behaviour, such as hoarding non-essential supplies. For example, in 1973, there was a shortage of many items in the USA. When talk show host Johnny Carson joked about people hoarding toilet paper, his audience somehow missed the joke. They took him seriously and created the pandemic reaction of hoarding toilet paper, despite there never being a real shortage. So, here we are, in 2020, forty-seven years after Carson joked about this behaviour, and people are reacting by hoarding toilet paper. This irrational type of survival behaviour is much more difficult to contain and eradicate.

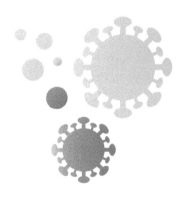

In his book, *Collapse: How Societies Choose to Succeed or Fail*, Jared Diamond uses the Law of the Commons (also termed the Tragedy of the Commons) to explain how society in Greenland collapsed after 450 years. As essential items became scarce, people hoarded whatever non-essential items they could until there was nothing left. They rationalized that if they did not take what limited resources were available, someone else would. So, they all died.

How people handle their fear is a key factor. How people handle other's fear is also an important factor. Do they react or respond? When people panic, they will often do what everyone else is doing without thinking it through, such as buying large supplies of non-essential items. Doing so gives them the illusion of control and a false sense of safety.

When something happens that people feel powerless to do anything about, the sensations of powerlessness are so uncomfortable, painful, and distressing that people will do anything to alleviate them. Buying vast amounts of unnecessary supplies gives them respite from these sensations. They believe they are doing something constructive. They get a break from the sensations that are creating havoc in their bodies and lives.

This brings us to what is really going on—people are behaving in ways to handle or *manage* the sensations they are experiencing.

This book is about educating people about the function of their brains, emotions, feelings, and sensations so that they can truly make what they want, need, and intend to happen. Control, in fact, becomes a non-issue—it is

just there, like breathing. How often do we think about breathing? Occasionally, we do, but mostly, we don't, and it just happens. We can count on it. We do not have to think about it.

Managing emotions and feelings is about focusing on the symptoms and not the cause of the symptoms.

In this book, you will learn what causes the symptoms and how to deal with the cause. It's not complicated. It's not difficult. In fact, it's much easier than you think. Humans were born knowing how to do it. You do not need to learn to meditate or practice yoga (although you may want to). You do not have to learn or join a program to *process* emotions.

It's about getting back to basics. However, to do so, we need to use the knowledge, awareness, and understanding we have about how to *process* the sensations and then practice the new behaviours until they become habitual.

CHAPTER ONE

Know Your Mind, Know Yourself

"Lose your mind and come to your senses." —Fritz Perls

Once living organisms come into existence, they strive to survive. Mother Nature wants each species to survive, so she programmed their DNA to help them succeed. The strong survive, and the weak die off. Many come into existence; some survive to procreate and pass on their genes. We arrived on this planet through no choice of our own. We did not decide to come into existence, but since we exist, we have an innate drive to survive, cope, and thrive.

SURVIVING: Food, clothing, attachment, shelter, sleep, connection, and safety. A lot of our thinking and feeling is geared toward survival. Survival is instinctive.

COPING: Lack of food, clothing, shelter, and dealing with difficult people, poor conditions, poor health, and lack of safety.

THRIVING: Living well, developing fully into all we can be intellectually, physically, and emotionally. We experience "flow," so we are creative, spontaneous, and productive. Our basic needs are met (food, clothing, shelter), and we have a support system in place, such as family and community, and are protected by and connected to others.

Newborn babies come into a complicated world in a very vulnerable state. From the moment they are conceived, they adapt to their environment in utero and after birth. In the first year, their brains grow the fastest; in the second year, the second-fastest; and the third year, the third-fastest. After that, their brain growth begins to slow down yet keeps growing until their mid-twenties. While the formation of neural pathways slows down, the brain continually adapts until death.

The developing brain is constantly adapting and adjusting to the environment—geographically, culturally, and socio-economically—and the current circumstances to which we are born (war/peace; feast/famine; quality of family/home; quality of mothering/care-taking). The brain develops neural pathways for every experience. In our early years, the brain creates neural pathways at an astonishing speed.

We are all shaped by the quality of life's conditions, circumstances, and the people who raise us, teach us, and interact with us. We are all shaped and influenced by our early experiences.

How do we know we exist? We know because we have receptors in our brains and bodies that pick up data through our senses—smell, sight, hearing, taste, and touch. These receptors gather data from the universe, detect or sense information through various ways, and convey it to the brain. There are also proprioceptors in our muscles that inform our brain where our body parts are so that we can coordinate them. According to Scottish genealogist Bruce Durie[1], humans have many more senses, at least twenty-one, meaning we have more senses than we thought.

Receptors bring all this sensory data to our brains so that our brains can create meaning. Why? So that we can survive. Survival is key to the evolution of the brain.

Instinctive Survival Behaviours

On Earth, no matter what the species, over thousands of years, basic methods of survival have become instinctual, that is, built into the DNA. The survival behaviours of Fight, Flight, and Freeze have developed over millions of years. The organisms that survived passed on their genes to the next generation, and so on.

These behaviours are so ingrained in our DNA that today, people's bodies and minds behave as though their fears are life-threatening.

---

[1] Article: Why you have at least 21 senses. NEW SCIENTIST Issue: 2484 January, 2005.

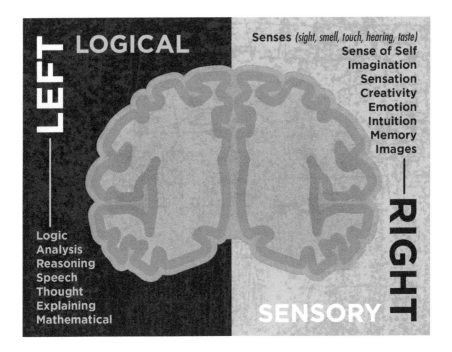

Left — Logical: Logic, Analysis, Reasoning, Speech, Thought, Explaining, Mathematical

Right — Sensory: Senses (sight, smell, touch, hearing, taste), Sense of Self, Imagination, Sensation, Creativity, Emotion, Intuition, Memory, Images

Human beings have been evolving for millions of years. To best understand how our minds and emotions function, let's look at the brain and its parts and how they work separately and together.

Human beings evolved separately from animals sometime around five to ten million years ago because the neocortex (the part of the brain that makes us human and differentiates us from animals) began to evolve and grow markedly larger.

At this time, the cavemen needed to leave the cave in search of food and materials. Therefore, because of their different roles, men's and women's brains developed somewhat differently.

The Two Hemispheres of the Brain

The brain has two hemispheres that co-exist side-by-side.[2] Each can function separately from the other, giving us two types of intelligence.

The Logical Brain

The Logical Brain is responsible for speech, understanding language, thought, mathematical and analytical reasoning, and aspects of our consciousness. The amazing facet of the Logical Brain is that there is no feeling or sensation in any part of it. It does not register fatigue, hunger, pain, sickness, or emotion. This hemisphere thinks very rapidly—thousands of thoughts per day.

---

[2]Joseph, R. Neuropsychiatry, Neuropsychology, and Clinical Neuroscience: Emotion Evolution, Cognition, Language, Memory, Brain Damage, and Abnormal Behaviour. 2nd ED. Williams & Wilkins. Baltimore, Maryland, USA, 1996

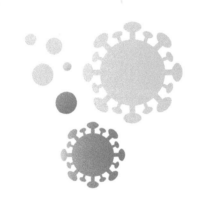

The Sensory Brain

The Sensory Brain is responsible for picking up all the non-verbal data around us, including the environment, our sense of self, our sense of others, and making sense of all the aspects of emotionality.

To be human is to be in a state of consciousness that enables one to think about one's own existence and experience and analyze the universe and all that is in it. Thought occurs in the Logical Brain, which has the capacity for language. Meanwhile, the Sensory Brain detects and registers all the sensory data with nerve endings designed/evolved to receive light, sound, touch, smell, taste, extrasensory, and other data from the universe.

The Logical Brain helped the cavemen survive. The cavemen needed to survive so that they could provide for the women and their clan. If they did not survive in the wild, their clan would die. The men who got sick, tired, emotional, or did not have the stamina to keep going, did not survive. The men who could stay in the Logical Brain were more likely to survive and get back to the clan. If they were tired, they did not feel tired. If they were injured, they did not feel pain. If they were terrified, they did not feel fear. If they were sick, they did not feel the symptoms. Because they stayed in their Logical Brain, they managed to keep going and get back to the clan. The cavemen who returned to the clan passed their genes onto their offspring, making the next generations stronger.

Meanwhile, the women stayed back at the caves and multi-tasked while the men were away. They cooked, skinned the animals, collected firewood, tended to the children, cleaned the home, and nurtured relationships. If they felt sick, they could lie down; if they were tired, they could rest; if they were hurt, they would feel pain. There

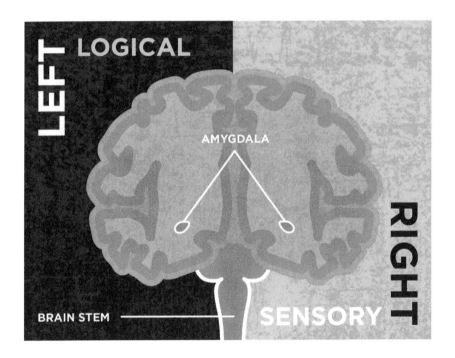

were times when the women needed to block out sensations and operate from thinking. This included times when they needed to haul water long distances, when animals stalked them, or when their shelter was threatened. However, this did not often happen, at least not for long periods of time.[3]

Today, we have more information than ever before on how the brain is structured and its different function. Magnetic Resonance Imaging (MRI) has allowed scientific research to be conducted on the brain, which is the most complicated organ in our bodies.

The Brain Stem

The brain stem, which is rarely talked about, keeps the body functioning. This process is called introception.[4] The brain stem supports the organism's basic functions. Many brainstem functions, such as walking, chewing, and breathing are performed reflexively, which does not require thinking or planning.[5]

The Amygdala—The Overseer

An important part of the brain is the amygdala. There are two amygdalae, one in each brain hemisphere, about the size of an almond, and they play a significant role in the brain's functioning.

---

[3] Joseph, R. Neuropsychiatry, Neuropsychology, and Clinical Neuroscience: Emotion Evolution, Cognition, Language, Memory, Brain Damage, and Abnormal Behaviour. 2nd ED. Williams & Wilkins. Baltimore, Maryland, USA, 1996.
[4] Feldman Barrett, L. How Emotions Are Made: The Secret Life of the Brain. 2017
[5] Joseph, R. Neuropsychiatry, Neuropsychology, and Clinical Neuroscience: Emotion Evolution, Cognition, Language, Memory, Brain Damage, and Abnormal Behaviour. 2nd ED. Williams & Wilkins. Baltimore, Maryland, USA, 1996

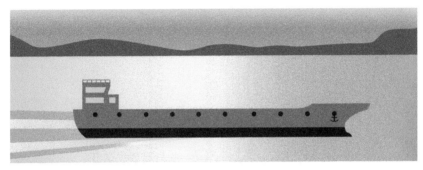

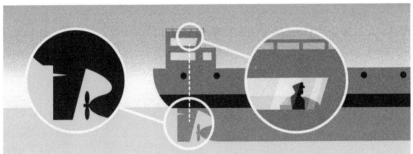

The amygdala is like the wheelhouse of a supertanker. Every part of a supertanker, above and below water, is connected to the wheelhouse. The wires, mechanisms, computers, and devices are needed to convey immense amounts of information to the central place on the ship. From the wheelhouse, the captain can control the whole ship.

If there is any danger, such as a fire, leak, breakdown, or other problem, the wheelhouse can detect it and attend to it immediately. The wheelhouse is always on alert for danger within the ship and beyond it.

The amygdala has the capacity and ability to constantly monitor the data coming in from the other parts of our body, including the senses, other parts of the brain, and the environment. It is on alert for internal and external danger.

In the time of the cavemen, the amygdala alerted the adrenal glands to pump adrenaline into the bloodstream when there was danger. The danger the cavemen experienced was often life-threatening, so the adrenaline fueled their muscles for the actions of Fight, Flight, or Freeze.

Today, humans still experience the Fight, Flight, and Freeze reactions. However, in many situations, the danger we experience is not life-threatening, yet the brain reacts and responds as though it is, i.e., losing one's job, failing an exam, losing a lover, or dealing with an abusive parent, spouse, boss, etc.

When children grow up in dangerous situations, experience difficult circumstances, or live in families that are not safe, their amygdalae are so used to being on alert and therefore so used to sending signals to the adrenal glands to pump adrenaline into the bloodstream that it is difficult for them to enjoy happy, carefree, and fun activities for any length of time. They develop many neural

pathways for vigilance and danger. For them, life is serious business. They are on alert. If they let their guard down, they often experience serious consequences. They usually suffer from nightmares and symptoms such as anxiety, numbness, and bedwetting. They have some neural pathways for play and fun, but not many. As adults, it is difficult for them to relax and feel calm. It's like a hot water tap that cannot be fully turned off.

Children who grow up in mostly happy, safe, loving families develop many neural pathways for living well. They will naturally *process* emotions as allowed and modelled by supportive parents, other family members, and their communities. This is what every child should be able to do growing up. This is what is natural and psychologically healthy.

The amygdala is also important in emotional and motivational functioning. It serves as the seat of social and emotional intelligence.[6] It is responsible for generating and maintaining mood. The amygdala also plays a role in sexual activity and sex drive. For its size, the amygdala has an immense role in human functioning, and its most crucial role is to coordinate the two brain hemispheres.

The brain can get overwhelmed by too much data. However, generally speaking, the more data we have, the more we make sense of our current situations and better decisions precipitate. By making better decisions, we are likely to survive, cope, and thrive. While the Logical Brain makes decisions, our decisions are informed by the experiences that stem from the Sensory Brain. Therefore, it is crucial to use both. This means we need to connect more with our Sensory Brain by getting in touch with our emotions, feelings, and sensations.

[6] Joseph, R. Neuropsychiatry, Neuropsychology, and Clinical Neuroscience: Emotion Evolution, Cognition, Language, Memory, Brain Damage, and Abnormal Behaviour. 2nd ED. Williams & Wilkins. Baltimore, Maryland, USA, 1996

Understanding the Brains—Logical Brain and Sensory Brain

People are strongly motivated to understand why and how they came to feel what they feel. Often, it helps to understand this, and it may even evoke positive change. However, understanding alone does not induce change because people do not know what else to do; they often get stuck in the Logical Brain re-analyzing and re-thinking with the hope/intent to get the change they seek. What they do not know is that understanding is *not necessary* for change.

The answer is to shift from thinking to sensing—to shift out of the Logical Brain by interrupting the thinking and focusing on the sensations in the body. Typically, people do not want to feel painful emotions because they are afraid of the *sensations* as they are intense and unpleasant.

I'm Okay as Long as I'm Busy

My client Inez came to see me in August 2020. She had been sexually abused as a young child by her father. She had never had treatment or help to heal this unhealed trauma. Instead, she had coped with it by developing a lifestyle that required her to stay in her Logical Brain. By staying in her Logical Brain, she could block out the memories and sensations of the abuse. She could never rest.

Inez had an extremely busy career as a real estate agent, which kept her occupied seven days per week. She was very good at what she did. When she took holidays, she travelled to different parts of the world. She scuba-dived on the Great Barrier Reef, zipped lined in Costa Rica, cycled through the wine counties in France, hiked Machu Picchu in Peru, etc. She lived an exciting life, always busy and active, and this was how she kept her "demons" (the unhealed trauma from her childhood) in check. As long as she was busy, she did not think of the past, and she did not feel the sensations that constitute a significant part of unhealed trauma.

Then COVID-19 hit.

Her lifestyle was impacted. The housing market dried up. She could not travel. She could not keep herself in her Logical Brain, and the memories and sensations in her Sensory Brain started breaking through her psychic wall and into her awareness.

That is when she sought therapy.

Self-Fulfilling Prophecy

My client Eugenie came to me in the spring of 2019. She was a wealthy widow in her seventies, living in a multi-million-dollar home in an upscale area of the city. She lived alone. She had arthritis, which made moving around difficult. Therefore, she had help in the form of cleaners who came once a week to clean her large home and helpers to help her get dressed and help her with meals. She had gardeners who kept the large grounds immaculate, and since there was always something that needed to be fixed, she often had handymen with whom to deal.

Eugenie lived in her Sensory Brain. She was always afraid of something. She worried excessively, ruminating about the same issues. Logic did not resonate with her. She suffered from many aches, pains, and illnesses. She had few friends and not much to do.

She had two children. One had died of a childhood illness, while the other was a son, unmarried, who was now in his late thirties. He was an actor who worked on and off. He did not live with her. Eugenie admitted that she had spoiled her son as a young child and teen and even in his adult years, occasionally giving him large sums of money.

Her concern in therapy was that she feared her son would have her committed so that he could have access to her money. We worked on her fears, most of which were irrational. I worked with her to develop strategies for dealing with her son. She was managing okay.

Then COVID-19 hit.

Eugenie's world was already small. During the COVID-19 lockdown, the people who typically helped her could not come into her home, and she could therefore not manage it herself. She did not go out except for doctor's appointments and appointments with me. She was terrified of catching the virus and dying alone.

The isolation because of COVID-19 exacerbated her fears and worry. She reported that people were coming into her home at night and moving her papers around. She then tipped over into paranoia, and the very thing she feared came to pass when one day, on a visit to her doctor, he had her committed.

Exercise

Let's get you out of your Logical Brain and into your Sensory Brain. Some people find it difficult to get into the Sensory Brain and notice the sensations in their bodies.

Let's start with the clothes on your body:

- How do you know that you are not naked?

- You know because you feel the sensations of the clothes on your body.

Now, let's focus on your feet:

- Do one foot at a time.

- Is your (left) foot bare, or are you wearing a sock?

- If it is, feel/sense the bareness.

- If you are wearing a sock, feel the sock on your foot. See if you can feel where the top of your sock stops and your leg begins. If your leg is bare, feel the bareness.

Now, shift to the other foot:

- Is your (right) foot bare, or are you wearing a sock?

- If it is, feel/sense the bareness.

- If you are wearing a sock, feel the sock on your foot. See if you can feel where the top of your sock stops and your bare skin begins. If your leg is bare, feel the bareness.

Continue doing this by going up your entire body until you reach the top of your head:

- Now, you are more aware of your body.

How to Help Others Help Themselves

Help people articulate their experience as specifically as possible:

- Listen for the person's *view* and *experience* of the facts, situation, circumstances, etc. Do *not* get caught up in the content.

- Keep your advice to yourself. People may say they want advice, but they don't because either they have already tried it or considered what you are suggesting and have rejected it, or they do not want to be told what to do.

- Be a sounding board. Reflect their views and experiences to them. Help people articulate what they are thinking and feeling. Often, that is all that is needed (i.e., do not judge, do not argue, do not play the Devil's Advocate).

Key Takeaways:

- Logical Brain = speech, understanding language, thought, mathematical and analytical reasoning, and aspects of our consciousness.

- Sensory Brain = non-verbal data around us, including the environment, our sense of self, our sense of others, and making sense of all the aspects of emotionality.

CHAPTER TWO

Feel Fully,
Feel More Alive

"Therefore let your soul exalt your reason to the height of passion, that it may sing; And let it direct your passion with reason, that your passion live through its own daily resurrection, and like the Phoenix rise above its own ashes." —Kalil Gibran

LOGICAL BRAIN	SENSORY BRAIN
THINK = LEFT	FEEL = RIGHT
LOGIC = LEFT	SENSE = RIGHT
= I think I am lonely	= I feel lonely
= Analysis of feelings	= Expression of feelings
= Makes decisions	= Decisions precipitate

The Logical Brain and the Sensory Brain each have their unique functions, and both are amazing at what they can do. They can work separately, and they can work together. When they work together, they create a third function, referred to here as synthesis and integration.

The Logical Brain and the Sensory Brain help us make the healthiest sense of our lives, which precipitates actions/behaviours that best fit our current circumstances.

The Sensory Brain, the limbic system, and the body create the emotions that human beings experience, while the Logical Brain analyzes the emotions.

LOGICAL BRAIN + SENSORY BRAIN = SYNTHESIS Integration of Facts & Sensation/Feelings

For example, as hydrogen and oxygen synthesize, water is precipitated; the same is true of different brain functions. As the Logical Brain data comes together with the Sensory Brain data, it creates (precipitates) new neural pathways with new/different sensations.

$$2H + 1O = H_2O$$

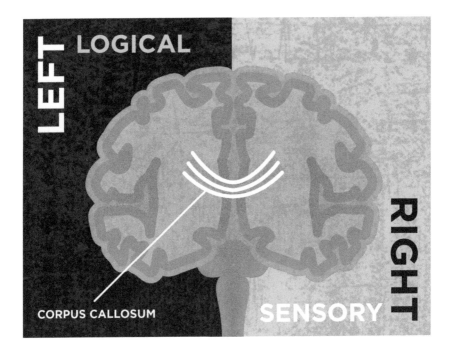

The Corpus Callosum—Connecting the Logical Brain and the Sensory Brain

The corpus callosum is a band of neurons that connect the Logical Brain and the Sensory Brain. The band of neurons is thinner in men compared to women. As mentioned in Chapter 1, the male and female brains developed differently based on the different tasks required for each sex's survival. To survive, cavemen needed to stay in the Logical Brain more often, while cavewomen could freely go back and forth between the Logical Brian and the Sensory Brain.

Another factor that shaped the human brain is the influence of culture. For centuries, society has discouraged men from displaying or expressing emotions other than anger. Most men usually get angry when they need to cry because it is socially acceptable for them to be angry and NOT socially acceptable for them to cry.

On the other hand, most women usually cry when they need to be angry because it is socially acceptable for them to cry and NOT socially acceptable for them to get angry.

It is my belief that cultural pressures shaped the male and female brains.

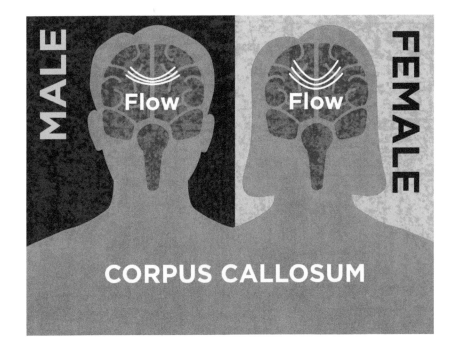

The metaphor of the doorway is used to convey the function of the corpus callosum. The corpus callosum is like a tunnel with a doorway that can be opened and closed, depending on the circumstances. The function is the same for both sexes, but for men, the doorway is narrow and more often closed, while for women, it's wider and more often opened. Therefore, it's easier for men to close it and more difficult for women.

When flow through the corpus callosum is blocked, the Logical Brain and Sensory Brain data cannot connect (synthesize); thus, new neural pathways cannot be formed. This can be helpful in many situations in the short term.

For example, breaking one's leg in a car accident and blocking the pain and trauma out (staying in the Logical Brain), but managing to get out of the car and walking to get help.

When the corpus callosum is open, it allows data flow to occur between the Logical Brain and the Sensory Brain. As the data comes together, it is synthesized, creating new neural pathways; thus, creating new perceptions, sensations, and experiences, which ultimately foster intellectual and emotional growth.

For example, after managing to get out of the car and walking to get help, the injured person eventually feels the pain of their broken leg and the trauma of the accident (reconnecting with the Sensory Brain) and can no longer walk on their injured leg.

The Difference Between *Processing* Emotions and *Managing* Emotions

Processing Emotions:

One notices unpleasant sensations in body.

One stays focused on the unpleasant sensations in the body.

One takes deep breaths.

One does NOT try to figure out "Why?"

One stays relaxed, breathes slowly.

One's sensations shift and change/often come in waves.

One stays calm and stays focused on sensations.

One's sensations shift and change/become less intense.

One stays calm and focuses on sensations.

One breathes through this awareness.

One's sensations have disappeared and are completely gone.

One's new sensations come into awareness.

Managing Emotions:

One notices unpleasant sensations in the body.

One shifts to the Logical Brain and asks "Why?"

One holds breath and / or breathes shallow.

One keeps trying to figure out "Why?"

One gets tense, muscles tighten.

One's sensations increase.

One worries about physical and mental health.

One's sensations increase in intensity and unpleasantness.

One gets more worried.

One focuses on a task to deflect from sensations.

One forgets about sensations.

One's sensations and worries leave awareness.

sensations come in waves

breathe with the waves

breathe through the sensations

Growing up, we learn to *manage* our physical sensations. We eat when we feel the sensations of hunger, drink when we feel the sensations of thirst, sleep when we feel the sensations of fatigue, etc. Often, we need to wait to set a time to do these familiar behaviours, but these needs must eventually be met.

The same is true of our emotions. They come from living life. We learn to express them at times that are natural and appropriate. Sometimes, we need to wait to express and *process* them when it is safe and appropriate.

The Physiology of Breathing

The breath is the key to the flow of data through the corpus callosum. Holding the breath and breathing shallow blocks the flow, while deeply breathing facilitates the flow.

The diaphragm is a muscle that divides the upper body from the lower body. When the diaphragm contracts, it creates space in the upper body, and our lungs draw in air.

When the diaphragm relaxes, the air is pushed out. This happens continuously without us having to think about it.

When something happens that we perceive to be dangerous or intense, positive or negative, we tend to hold our breath and/or breathe shallow. By doing so, we block the transmission of logical and sensory data through the corpus callosum.

Jumping up and down from excitement and happiness helps to *process* positive sensations because breathing is increased during this vigorous activity. With painful and difficult sensations, such as grief and loss, people tend to

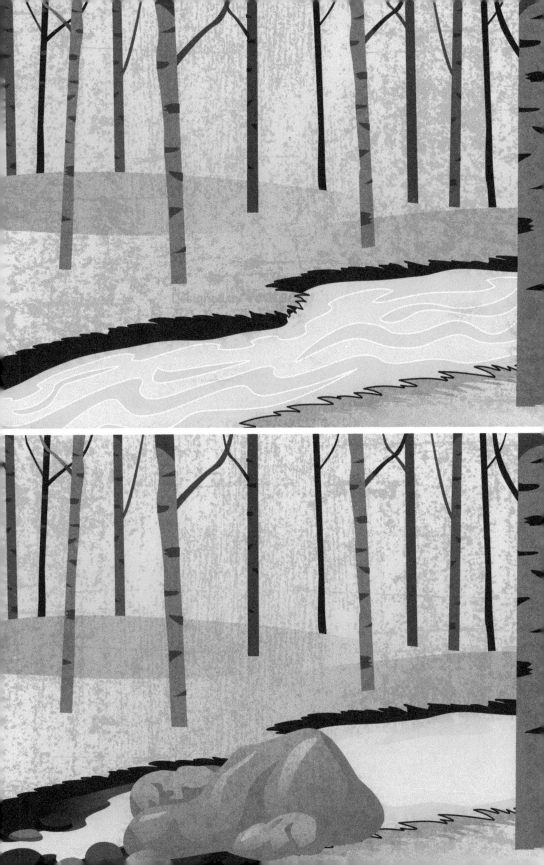

curl up, choke off sobs, and be less active, which blocks the *processing* of sensations.

The sensations of feelings that are not *processed* build up over time, highjacking our personal energy. Part of this personal energy is used to block/hold back the natural energy we possess, which flows and just "is."

Consider that human emotion is like a creek that is constantly flowing. If left alone, the water naturally flows. Sometimes, it overflows, and other times, it is almost dry. Then, a dam is built to hold back the natural flow of water. As the water level begins to rise, it puts more pressure on the dam. The water is now *managed*. However, if enough water is not allowed to flow, the water gets higher, and the pressure against the dam is now stronger. Therefore, the dam must be built higher and stronger to hold back the rising water, which requires more energy from the builders. Ultimately, the dam cannot be built any higher, and the water begins to spill over the top.

The water is the person's natural energy in the emotional form. If the emotion is not allowed to flow, the emotion will build up. It takes personal energy to block or stop the flow of emotion. Now, the person's energy is split—there is the natural flow of the emotions that needs *processing*, and there is the blocking of the *processing*. This leads to inner conflict and impacts one's relationship with one's self. The organism's natural emotional energy presses against the psychic structure created to block the flow. Over time, more and more of a person's energy is needed to *manage* the emotions. This means the person has less and less energy available to live life.

STACK
of
COINS

Lost Keys

Missed the Bus

Didn't Get
the Promotion

Splashed by a Car

She Doesn't Feel
the Same Way
About Me

Phone Broke

Eventually, something will give. The person will either live a limited life or have an emotional breakdown; they will either implode or explode. The part of the person that blocks the emotion will start to crumble and even collapse entirely, or the emotion will begin to spill over, and emotional expression will be in excess of what the situation requires—such as crying at work or outbursts of anger over small incidents, such as spilt milk. This leads to emotional exhaustion and an inability to function, which is often what a mid-life crisis involves. A person's way of operating in the world developed over time no longer works, but they do not yet have a new way of being; therefore, they stay the same. They use so much energy to *manage* their emotions that there is not enough energy to function in daily life. What they need to do is to stay with the sensations of the emotions by breathing.

The
CYCLE

EXPLOSION
(Outward)

PEACE | TENSION BUILDS | FATIGUE | STRESS | NEGATIVE THOUGHTS | BODY SENSATIONS | RED FLAG

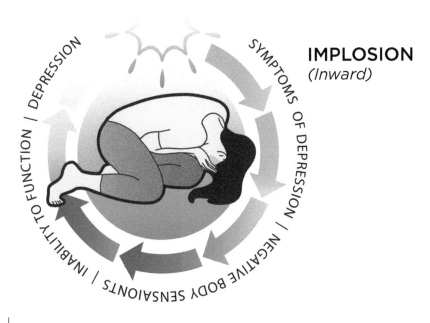

IMPLOSION
(Inward)

SYMPTOMS OF DEPRESSION | NEGATIVE BODY SENSAIONTS | INABILITY TO FUNCTION | DEPRESSION

Built into every dam are sluice gates to regulate and control the flow of water. If there is too much water, the sluice gates are opened, and more water can flow through. This alleviates pressure on the dam so that it can hold strong. In this sense, a person can find the sluice gates in their own dam and begin to open them up by breathing while focusing on the sensations as the emotions flow through. Before the water spills over, a person can open the sluice gates and let some water (emotions) through, meaning they can begin to *process* their emotions; thus, developing a new way of being.

WHAT IS, IS.

Sometimes, during this shift, the biggest temptation is to avoid feeling the sensations (a twinge, some nausea, a slight headache, etc.) and immediately shift back into the Logical Brain and figure out why they are feeling this way. However, it does not matter why! It also does not matter who, what, when, where, or how. What matters is that they are having these sensations and need to stay with them. What is, is. When we stay with the sensations and breathe into them, we are *processing* them; we are creating new neural pathways that precipitate new sensations, and, therefore, we evolve emotionally and change in a healthy and positive way. As we reconnect with our bodies, we feel more connected to ourselves.

I'm Terrified I'm Going to Lose My Baby

Charlie, a client I had worked with several years ago, reached out to me for therapy regarding his high anxiety. He worked as a mechanic on airplanes. He had been off work for four weeks and was afraid of losing his job. Because of COVID-19, we were unable to meet in person, so we met using videoconferencing.

His nine-month-old infant son has had respiratory problems since birth. Charlie said he had spent numerous nights at the hospital with him and constantly feared losing him.

When the COVID-19 pandemic started, Charlie became even more vigilant about his son's health. Charlie was terrified his son would catch the virus. Even though he was taking all the necessary precautions, Charlie had become hyper-alert and could not work. Charlie was scaring himself with thoughts and images of his baby getting sick and dying. He was also afraid it would be his fault.

I worked with Charlie to realize what he was doing and to take responsibility for it. I taught him the difference between valid fear and irrational fear. I then coached him to interrupt his negative thoughts by staying with the sensations of fear and panic. I helped him focus on the sensations of fear as he experienced them and breathe through the waves as they rose, crested, and receded. As he did this, the sensations subsided. As the quality of the sensations became less intense and uncomfortable, Charlie calmed down and became more rational.

It took several weeks for him to develop the habit of breathing through the sensations of fear, but once he did, he felt in control, and he could return to work.

Exercise

Breathing Exercise:

Start with five seconds, then increase the time with each session.

- Pay attention to your breathing.

- Be aware of breathing in and notice the cool air entering your nostrils.

- Be aware of the warm air exiting your nostrils.

- Notice any sensations in your body. Do not try to change anything. There is no need to name or identify anything. Just *sense*.

- Be curious. What is, is.

- Catch yourself thinking.

- Shift to your body and notice the sensations. At first, you may not feel anything, so let it be. Let go of thinking about it.

- Stay with the numbness.

- As you continue to interrupt your thinking and shift to your body, you will notice sensations.

How to Help Others Help Themselves

Help others shift from thinking to sensing by asking about their feelings:

Ask questions that revolve around their feelings and not about the facts. The purpose of the questions is to elicit the sensations the person had experienced in the past and is experiencing in the present. People usually respond to these questions with explanations and more facts. That's okay; keep listening and inquiring about their feelings. When they articulate their feelings, they become more aware, which they will find to be helpful.

Examples of questions (note: none of the questions or statements below mention any facts):

- When that happened, what impact did it have on you?

- When they said that to you, how did you feel?

- What was that like for you?

- How do you know when you feel disappointed? Where in your body are you experiencing sensations?

- When you found out, what was that like for you?

- Where in your body did you feel that?

- Did it feel more like a pain or an ache?

Examples of statements:

- Help me understand how you coped with that.

- Once again, run that by me.

- Walk me through how you felt during that. I want to know what it was like for you.

Key Takeaways:

- The corpus callosum is a band of neurons that join the Logical Brain and the Sensory Brain.

- Deeply breathing facilitates the flow of Logical data and Sensory data through the corpus callosum.

- New neural pathways form by synthesis and integration, creating new sensations.

- Holding the breath prevents the formation of new neural pathways.

CHAPTER THREE

Breathe and Connect

"Awareness is the key to change." —Anonymous

Sometimes, when we hear something, see something, or think something, we hold our breath without realizing it. We go into the Logical Brain and think about it, question it, and analyze it, often disconnecting from our bodies. We often spend excessive amounts of time thinking, worrying, weighing the pros and cons, and scaring, doubting, and beating ourselves up. There is nothing wrong with thinking. But over-thinking, over-analyzing, and being too logical is not productive or healthy. What is important is the quality of our thinking. By changing the quality of our thinking (positive rather than negative), the meaning changes.

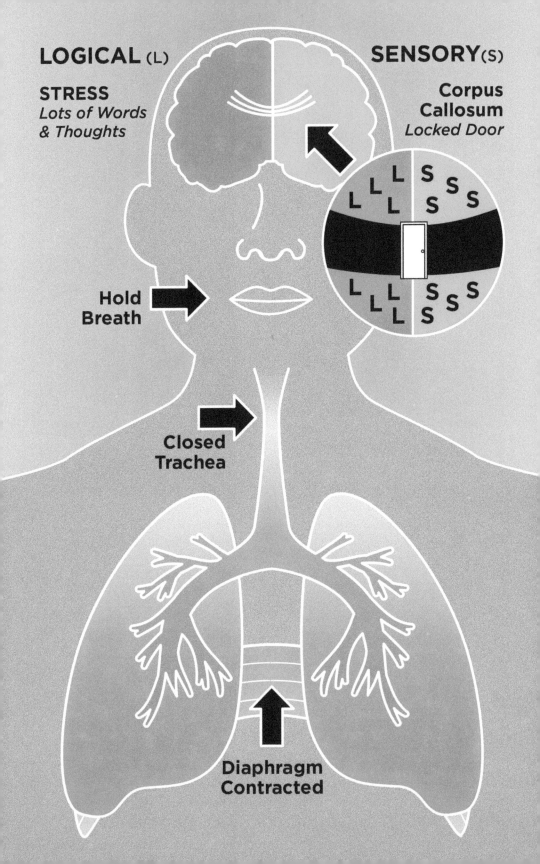

You can get into the Sensory Brain and stop over-thinking and analyzing everything by interrupting the Logical Brain.

Holding the breath and breathing shallow blocks the expression of emotions. This is a result of our Fight, Flight, Freeze response, and this happens when a person is afraid and adapts by *managing* emotions; they feel sensations and do not know what to do with them. The sensations increase because they cannot be *processed,* and then the person becomes more frightened, increasing the sensations even more and creating a vicious cycle. Fatigue, disappointment, discouragement, and other experiences give wear and tear on the person, and, therefore, people are more likely to meltdown or explode from the backlog of emotions.

Some people will often try indulging in all sorts of things to get respite from the sensations, like food, alcohol, medication, marijuana, etc. This might work, but not always. They might believe that the emotions need to be *managed* because they are always there in some form or another.

People are afraid of losing control if they stop *managing* their emotions. This is because they don't understand what is going on and how the Logical and Sensory brains work. People are ignorant about how their brains function. They believe there is only one way to think—the way they do. If there is no awareness of how the brain works, there is no change. "I'm stuck with the way my brain works," or "I'm stuck with how I feel emotionally."

People often feel they are a victim of their emotions. To them, emotions seem unpredictable and confusing, making it harder to *manage* them. However, when people take responsibility for the emotions they experience, they can take charge of them. When people understand how

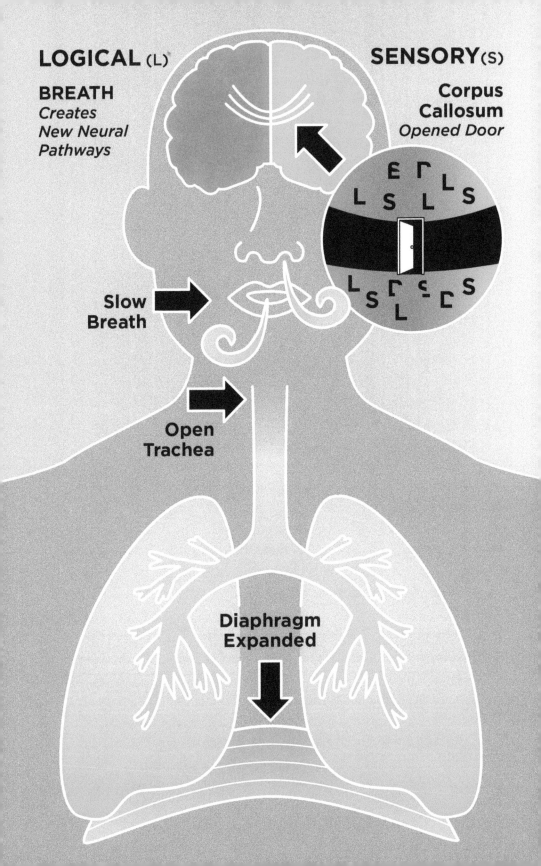

their brains work and how to *process* emotions, they feel empowered and are not afraid of their brains (or emotions) anymore. As people experience positive changes from *processing* the sensations, control becomes a non-issue, just like breathing. People need to be re-taught what to do instead of *managing* their emotions.

We are born knowing how to *process* emotions. Without language, infants have no thoughts, but they experience a bundle of sensations. Babies are born knowing how to cry because it is instinctual. They cry to communicate their needs—hunger, fatigue, comfort, connection, and attachment. The purpose of crying is to get their caregiver's attention. If the caregiver does not come and does not provide the child with what he/she needs, the baby may not develop healthy ways of being.

When parents and other family members are happy, cuddly, and pay attention to their children, their children experience the sensations of pleasure, love, and connection. When they are distressed by events, such as interaction with an angry sibling, a frightening experience, or a parent leaving home, they feel the sensations of discomfort and pain, and their natural tendency is to cry. They cry fully and deeply in waves of sobs and wails that gradually get smaller until they are gone. Once they are gone, the child recovers quickly to their natural state. It often takes only a few minutes.

Crying is a genuine response to a situation that is distressing or overly positive, such as a child's disappointment when their toys are taken away or waves of gratitude when receiving a much-needed gift of money. The crying that is being referred to here is not in any way manipulative. Manipulative crying is a different type of crying, which both children and adults often use.

It's Okay If I Cry

As two-year-old Joey was running his toy car on the furniture, he accidentally knocked over his mom's coffee. She yelled at him as she rushed to clean it up. He was startled and frightened by what happened. His mother's tone and facial expression distressed him. He cried fully and deeply. His little tummy expanded and contracted as his breath came in deep sobs. His cries came in waves. At first, his cries were loud and long until they became less intense. Gradually, his cries subsided and came to a natural halt. He quickly and easily went back to happily playing with his toy cars.

Not all expression of emotion involves crying. Sometimes, the expression of emotion may be sensations of fear/terror or intense sensations of love. The universe operates in waves, such as light waves, sound waves, heat waves, radio waves, etc. Emotions come in waves. An emotion wells up, crests, and then recedes. Then another wave—a smaller wave—rises, crests, and recedes. If the waves are not interrupted, they continue as long as the emotion lasts until there are no more waves, just like the waves reaching the ocean shore; they dissipate and are gone.

The breath is an integral part of this wave pattern. As the wave of sensations increases, the breath allows the flow of logical and sensory data through the corpus callosum. As the different types of data synthesize and integrate, new neural pathways form. The sensations are then *processed*, and there is nothing left to *manage*.

When people can fully express their emotions by breathing through the sensations, their personal energy stays aligned. People feel grounded because they stay connected to themselves. They can trust their emotions because they experience the sensations fully, meaning they do not avoid them. Because they can feel the range of sensations from peaceful to agitated and from ecstatic to despair, they feel a strong sense of aliveness. Thus, they heal from any emotional trauma they might have gone through or are currently experiencing.

As mentioned in Chapter 2, people learn to *manage* their emotions by holding their breath and/or breathing shallow, as this prevents the waves of sensations from cresting and receding. Here, part of the person's energy is trying to flow, and part is blocking the flow. The person's energy is opposed.

Interoception = Sensations = Affect

KEY

■ Terror

|■| Fear/Insecurity

|■| Safety/Security

[■] Absolute Safety

/WW\ Ecstasy/Elation

/\/\/\ Happiness/Joyfulness

vvv Sadness/Remorse

—— Deep Saddness/Grief/Loss

⟷ Extreme Disgust/Repulsion

◇ Disgust/Repulsion

✕ Attraction

✖ Desire

◎ Deep Shame

◉ Slight Shame/Humiliation/Embarrassment

▲ Pride

⩕ Extreme Pride

∞ Neutrality

As we grow up, we get messages about crying and other expressions of emotion from our family members, community, and culture. Somewhere along the path of growing up, children learn that expressing emotions is either welcome or not. Lucky are the children raised in homes and cultures where the expression of emotions is allowed and encouraged. They are coached on how to *process* their emotions by parents who know how to do the same. They develop many neural pathways for natural expression, enabling them to stay connected to themselves and others. Their energy is aligned and flowing in the same direction, and they can live life to the fullest.

Where Does It All Go Wrong?

What happens when families and cultures do not welcome the expression of emotion or only allow certain emotions to be expressed?

Parents either express or don't express their emotions. If parents suppress their emotions, their babies and toddlers copy them as they copy most things their parents or others do, such as mannerisms. When some children are very young, adults often scare, threaten, or train them to shut down the natural sequence of expression. When children are scared, they instinctively hold their breath and/or breathe shallow until their fear passes. They feel the sensations of terror, endure them, and try to survive them, or they freeze until the danger passes. They build many neural pathways for blocking and managing their emotions. This becomes a way of being—a habit—that helps them survive childhood. The problem is that they typically maintain this way of being into adulthood, and they often pass it onto their children.

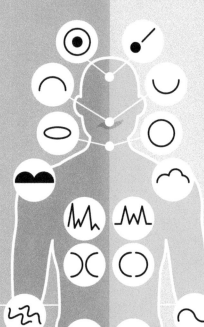

KEY

⊙ Migraine

⌒ Frown/
Pursed Lips/
Gritting Teeth

⬭ Lump in Throat/
Constricted
Trachea

◖ Shoulders Heavy/
Stiff/Tight

Λ Racing Heart/Chest
Tightness

)(Diaphragm Tightness/
Shallow/Rapid Breath

⋈ Intestinal Issues, Cramps

ʮ Negative Sexual
Urges/Sensations/Addiction

⌇ Shaky/Tingly/Numb Arms

⌇ Shaky/Tingly/Numb Legs

✳ Cold/Sore/Numb Feet

Therapeutic ╱•
Headache

Smile/ ⌣
Relaxed Mouth

Voice/Laughter/ ◯
Relaxed Trachea

Relaxed/Light ⌣
Shoulders

Positive Excitement/ ᴧᴧ
Normal Heartbeat

Deep/Rhythmic Breath ()

Positve Butterflies/ ❧
Good Digestion

Positive Sexual ✳
Urges/Sensations

Relaxed Arms ∿

Strong/Balanced Legs ⊟

Warm/Steady Feet ◇

Parents and other adults treat children in many different ways when they are uncomfortable expressing their emotions. They often get angry. They may shame, blame, judge, embarrass, humiliate, deflect, divert, minimize, stone-wall, or name-call children—directly and indirectly—sending messages that expressing emotion is not acceptable and/or not tolerated. In turn, children assume they are bad.

When children are distressed, some parents make the situation worse by becoming more emotional than their children. Children learn that things get worse when they express emotion, so they shut themselves down. Children need their parents to be okay, so they may hide their emotions, often pretending they are okay when they are not. This too becomes a habit in childhood as they develop many neural pathways for blocking and shutting off. In adulthood, it becomes so familiar that it seems natural, but it's not.

I Don't Matter

Dina and Ruben sought counselling after many months of COVID-19 restrictions. Dina had lost her job at the spa, and Ruben was working from home. They had been struggling with their relationship for some time.

As I worked with them, I identified the problem in their dynamic. When Ruben would approach Dina with a relational problem, she would get upset and start crying. Ruben would then comfort and console her, reassuring her that everything between them was fine, even though it wasn't. In this way, Ruben never got his relational needs addressed,

In our sessions, their dynamic would play out.

One day, when Ruben was comforting Dina, he experienced an epiphany—this was like his relationship with his mother. He said that as a child, whenever he got upset, his mother would feel sick, and he would have to take care of her. He learned to put himself aside and pretend he was okay so that she wouldn't get "sick" and he wouldn't get stuck looking after her. He frequently felt he didn't matter. He was now unconsciously playing out this dynamic with his wife.

This was new information for Ruben. It helped him understand why he often felt invisible and unacknowledged in the relationship. By recognizing what he was experiencing, I validated his experience. I then shifted the focus to Dina to explore her part in their dynamic.

Common Dynamic

When one partner gets flooded with intense, unpleasant sensations and cannot stay present when the couple interacts, it eventually results in the other partner concluding, "I do not matter."

This is a common dynamic between couples, and it can play out in different ways.

The partner who cannot stay present has few neural pathways for intimacy and closeness. This typically happens when childhood relationships with parents, grandparents, siblings, and other close relationships have been or remain difficult.

When men lack neural pathways for intimacy and closeness, they become flooded with intense, unpleasant sensations when approached by their partners to resolve emotional problems. They often push their partners away and treat their partners with contempt or by getting angry. They cannot stay present and engaged with their partners, so their partners feel that they *do not matter.*

When women lack neural pathways for intimacy and closeness, they tend to blame themselves, believing something is wrong with them when approached by their partners to resolve emotional problems. They often shut down and frequently get physically ill. They cannot stay present and engaged with their partners, so their partners feel that they *do not matter.*

When relationships are new, there is a lot of goodwill and love, so partners stop trying to get their needs met and instead shift their focus to comforting and reassuring their partners. Over time, this pattern repeats, and the result is the same: the partner cannot stay present and engaged; thus, the connection is lost.

UNPLEASANT

PLEASANT

KEY

Unpleasant	Pleasant
Migraine	Therapeutic Headache
Frown/ Pursed Lips/ Gritting Teeth	Smile/ Relaxed Mouth
Lump in Throat/ Constricted Trachea	Voice/Laughter/ Relaxed Trachea
Shoulders Heavy/ Stiff/Tight	Relaxed/Light Shoulders
Racing Heart/Chest Tightness	Positive Excitement/ Normal Heartbeat
Diaphragm Tightness/ Shallow/Rapid Breath	Deep/Rhythmic Breath
Intestinal Issues, Cramps	Positve Butterflies/ Good Digestion
Negative Sexual Urges/Sensations/Addiction	Positive Sexual Urges/Sensations
Shaky/Tingly/Numb Arms	Relaxed Arms
Shaky/Tingly/Numb Legs	Strong/Balanced Legs
Cold/Sore/Numb Feet	Warm/Steady Feet

When people naturally access, express, and *process* their emotions, they behave in congruent ways. Depending on the context of a situation or their life circumstances, the emotion they experience and express will mostly be appropriate. However, even when people are congruent, they sometimes make mistakes, although less often, and the mistakes they make are less grave. Plus, they are better at repairing any damage.

To some extent, we all *manage* our emotions. Some people seem to be unable to *manage* their emotions and instead spill their emotions all over others. Others *manage* their emotions to such an extent that they seem like robots or humanoids.

Emotional Containers

We all develop a style of how we express and *manage* our emotions. The style in which we do so is influenced by how safe or unsafe we felt growing up. Some people have a rigid style, while others have an overly lax one. Someone with a rigid style represses their emotions to such an extent that they no longer feel the emotions themselves, making it hard for others to connect with them, whereas someone with an overly lax style can burden others by spilling their emotions onto them.

The Therapeutic Container

A person can act as a therapeutic container for someone else's emotions. For example, as a therapist, I provide a therapeutic container for my clients by creating a safe environment and connecting with them. In the process, I let

Jot down your ideas,
memories, sensations.

clients know they are in control and they do not have to do (or not do) anything they don't want to do. Furthermore, I must provide an environment where what my clients say and do remains confidential (except for information I am required to report by law—at the risk of danger to themselves or others).

Occasionally, early in therapy, new clients tell me that they trust me. In these instances, I inform them that it is too early to trust me and that they need to let me earn their trust. This is to teach them to have stronger boundaries to protect themselves from me and others.

Often, clients are not truthful at first. However, this is part of the process of building the therapeutic relationship. When they trust me and are ready to face what they need to face, they start speaking their truth.

When clients experience safety and connect with me, they begin to share their stories and express their emotions. They begin to let go of their containers and begin to allow me to be a container for them. When they let go, they can feel their emotions more deeply. I listen intently, support and encourage them, and validate their emotions and experiences.

I educate my clients about emotions, I reframe the content, and I fully engage in the process with them. Often, when clients experience deep emotional pain, I coach them to breathe through the waves of sensations. Sometimes, I want to facilitate their *processing* by sitting beside them and rubbing their back. I always ask for permission to do this. I let them know that they can tell me to stop at any time. This is the only time the container becomes physical. In this way, I am providing a therapeutic container for them.

One of the problems of COVID-19 restrictions is that I cannot approach the client as per social distancing measures. Furthermore, videoconferencing does not allow

me to do this. So, when I feel the urge to connect, I tell them that if it weren't for the COVID-19 restrictions, I would ask for permission to sit beside them and rub the center of their back. They are often grateful to know that I care about connecting with them.

In this healing process, people need to let go of their containers to go to the depth of their feelings and the intensity of their sensations. They need someone to trust and someone who is emotionally strong to "hold them" while they go through the process. It is very scary to go into the depths of despair (or other heavy emotion) alone. If we are with loved ones who are not solid themselves, we tend to hold ourselves back because we want to protect them from our emotional pain or because we know they can't handle it. Thus, we put our pain aside to look after them.

As children grow up, they develop emotional containers; they are not born with them intact. They need to develop them over time. They have urges and impulses that they learn to control, and often, they need their parents to be their emotional containers.

Sometimes, they need the emotional container to be physical, like when a father holds his extremely distraught son. How and when parents contain their children's emotions shapes the development of the child. When parents contain in a firm and loving way, children feel safe, loved, and that they matter. When parents contain in a harsh way, children feel unsafe, unloved, and that they do not matter. A child's natural spirit can be nourished and cherished, or it can be crushed and annihilated.

Healthcare Burnout

Kamila has been a client of mine intermittently for about ten years. She works as a nurse in a large hospital. When Kamila came in with her husband for a couple's session, I quickly realized that she was not herself. Instead of focusing on her marital relationship, she talked about the patients in her ward, saying she was concerned about their level of care.

I could tell she was exhausted but did not realize it. She looked and acted like a zombie. I reflected back to her, "You seem exhausted." She ignored my feedback and kept talking about the drop in the level of care at the hospital. I continued to listen to her and kept reflecting back to her, "You seem tired." She continued to focus on her concerns at the hospital. By the sixth time I caringly told her that she seemed exhausted, she finally broke down and started sobbing deeply. I suggested that her husband, who was concerned and shocked by the depth of her crying, put his hand on the middle of her back and gently rub it in small circles. He willingly complied. I then continued to reflectively listen to Kamila about her concern for her patients as I knew how important it was to her. She needed me, or at least someone, to validate her concern. As I did that, she let go and sobbed to the depths. Typically, she'd act as her own emotional container, but in this case, she did not need to because she knew I was there and could handle her deep emotion. I facilitated her expression of emotion as she cried through the waves of sensations.

At the end of the session, I told her I would contact her doctor and recommend that she take time off. She looked at me through her fatigue with relief in her eyes. I reassured her that I would tell her doctor that I was not worried about her level of care for her patients but that I was concerned she would risk her own physical and emotional health by taking care of others.

I told her husband that she would be exhausted after our session and for the next few weeks, so he would need to ensure that she got a lot of rest. He looked relieved as well as he knew she was overtired, but he was at a loss of what to do.

I contacted her family physician, and he put her on medical leave for four weeks. She is back at work again now and is doing okay.

The Importance of Having a Support System

For any of us, too much thinking inside our heads can lead to distortion. Sometimes, even saying what you think out loud without anyone hearing helps develop awareness. It helps to recognize distortion and/or healthy thinking/ideas. Having someone to talk to and use as a sounding board is very helpful. Talking to someone you trust to keep what you say/think in confidence will help you go deeper within yourself since you don't have to protect yourself. In addition, doing this work with a competent therapist who has your best interests at heart supports and encourages permanent therapeutic change.

You and anyone in your support system need to know that shifting from *managing* the sensations of emotions to *processing* the sensations of emotions takes time. However, once *processing* becomes a habit, it goes more quickly. Getting there may take some time because we hate to let go of the ways of being that helped us survive our childhood and even part of adulthood.

When people are emotionally healthy, they can be their own containers in constructive ways because they know how to *process* emotions. They typically do not need anyone to hold them or be a container for them emotionally—they eventually learn to do this for themselves through practice. However, it can still feel wonderful to be held emotionally and/or physically by a loved one or trusted friend.

Exercise

Connect with yourself at the depths and go to the edges and come back. Make sure to find an appropriate time and place to access your emotions so that you will not be interrupted.

- Shift out of the Logical Brain.

- Focus on your breath.

- Take your time (the Sensory Brain works more slowly than the Logical Brain).

- Imagine your pain as a dark blob or mass.

- Allow yourself to go to the edges of the mass.

- Allow the painful sensations to come more into your awareness.

- Breathe into the sensations for three to five seconds.

- Now, let the mass float away.

- Breathe.

- Rest.

- Repeat for ten seconds.

- Now, let the sensations float away.

- Breathe.

- Repeat for fifteen seconds.

- Stop when you want or before it gets to be too much, and plan another time to heal yourself.

Every time you do this, you will be able to go deeper and deeper. As you *process* the emotional pain, the mass will become smaller, and it will become easier until your personal energy is aligned.

How to Help Others Help Themselves

Comforting a person in emotional pain by rubbing their back:

- Only offer to rub someone's back if you want to and if you feel okay doing so.

- Let the distressed person know that you want to rub their back and say, "I want to sit beside you and rub the center of your back. Would you be okay with this?"

- Let the person know that if they are uncomfortable, they can tell you to stop.

- Once permission is obtained, sit next to them and slowly rub the center of their back (DON'T touch them anywhere else, i.e., stroke their hair, the sides of their body, their lower back, etc.).

- Ensure the person has access to tissues, but let them handle their physical expression on their own.

- Check with them to see if they want you to continue rubbing their back and move away if they don't. "Are you okay with me still rubbing your back?"

- Eventually, say to them, "I'm going to stop now. Are you okay with that?"

- If they are okay, move away. If not, continue.

- At some point, it will come to a natural end.

Be patient when you do this, as it can take a while. If at some point you need to go or you've had enough, you can inform the person that you are going to stop.

Key Takeaways:

- Emotions come in waves.

- Breathing through the sensations of emotions is the key to *processing* them.

- It's important to develop one's emotional container.

CHAPTER FOUR

Manage Less, Process More

"Let go of the outcome." —Anonymous

Oh! Now I Know What to Do

Giving birth to my first child left me feeling physically and emotionally exhausted for the first time in my life. After a complicated birth, I came home from the hospital and expected to carry on just as I had before. I was hyper-vigilant with my new baby and was sleep-deprived. About ten days later, I broke down sobbing and couldn't stop. I didn't know what was happening to me. Eventually, I realized I was experiencing total exhaustion. Of course, I felt exhausted, but since I hadn't felt that way before, I didn't know what I was feeling at first.

What that first experience of exhaustion taught me is that there are cues, in the form of sensations, that I can now use to monitor my degree of fatigue. I learned that when my left eyelid starts twitching, I know I'm tired, and I need to rest. If I'm more tired, I get a specific form of nausea. When I get these sensations, I know I must rest, or I can't function properly.

Understanding what these sensations mean has proved helpful. I use them as my guide to know when I need to rest so that I never get to the point of exhaustion again.

It's normal to feel something we've never felt before and not recognize it. We learn about specific emotions from others by talking about them, from reading books, listening to podcasts, and watching movies and TV. It's one thing to know something intellectually, yet entirely another to know it experientially. The more we can recognize, understand, and feel sensations, the better they can serve as our guide.

Most people do not understand emotions. They do not know how they are created. They tend to think they are arbitrary and unpredictable. People talk about their emotions as if they are conditions or a state-of-being. For example, "My anxiety is so high I can't go out tonight." Sometimes they even see them as illnesses. For example, "I've been suffering from depression for half my life." They do not realize that anxiety and depression are symptoms of their way of being in life. They are *managing* the symptoms instead of addressing the cause of their symptoms. They see doctors in hopes of getting help, but they often just get medications to treat their symptoms rather than the cause of their symptoms.

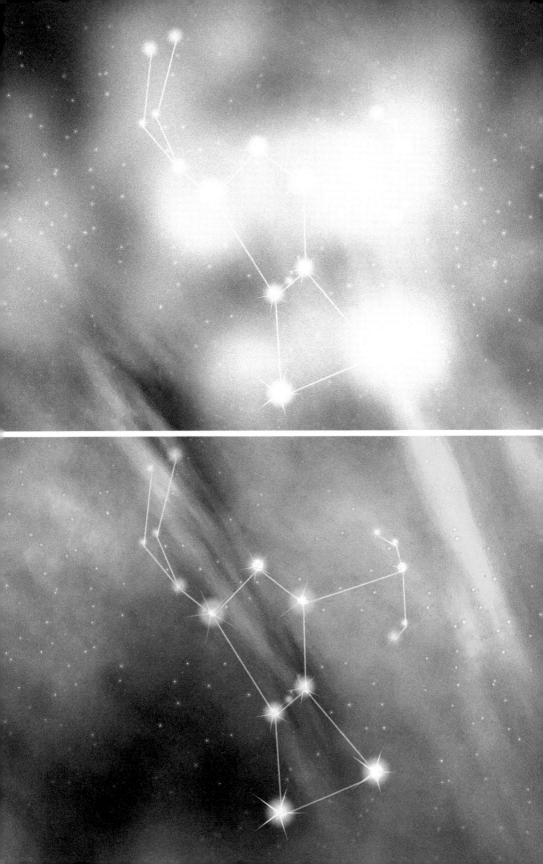

The Oxford dictionary defines emotion as:

- a strong feeling deriving from one's circumstances, mood, or relationships with others.

- an instinctive or intuitive feeling as distinguished from reasoning or knowledge.

The definition above does not include any mention of sensations in regard to emotions; however, I believe that sensations are at the root of emotional *processing*.

We can experience a range of different emotions, also called feelings. Some of these include happy, calm, peaceful, angry, abandoned, powerless, out-of-control, hopeless, irritated, shameful, cozy, loved, connected, delighted, spiritual, hopeful, lustful, goofy, detached, ecstatic, dreamy, inspired, hurt, and many more.

Some emotions are common, such as sadness, hurt, happiness, embarrassment, and excitement, while others are rarer, such as ecstasy, despair, emotional exhaustion, and abject terror. We experience each emotion on a level of intensity, ranging from slight to intense.

Emotions Are like Constellations of Stars in the Sky

To understand emotions, I look to the stars. There are millions of stars in the sky. No matter where we are in the universe, the stars stay in the same place, even if our view or perspective of them is different. Travellers have used stars to help guide them on their journeys for centuries. To understand and talk about the stars, we have organized them into groups called constellations and have

Breathe through the sensations.

given them individual names—Big Dipper, Small Dipper, Orion, Cassiopeia. The good news is that we do not need to know everything about the universe to use the stars as our guides.

Naming the Constellations of Emotions

- Emotions: umbrella of feeling states.

- Feelings: feeling states comprising specific constellations of sensations.

- Sensations: sensory data from our senses—sight, hearing, smell, taste, and touch (this includes images and memories).

We have proprioceptors in our muscles, which inform us where our body parts are. We have extrasensory perception, often called the sixth sense, which helps us detect information from the universe through telepathy or clairvoyance.

I define emotion as:

- a unique constellation of sensations grouped together and experienced in the Sensory Brain, limbic system, and body.

- a feeling state that informs us: a) we are alive, that we are living, breathing organisms, and b) we are humans and not robots.

- intuitive or instinctive as opposed to logical and rational.

Joy

Years ago, I lived in a home and had my office in one half of my garage. One day I was seeing clients, going back and forth between the house and garage. One time, as I was going out to the garage, I was struck by the beauty of the yellow daffodils planted outside the garage. They filled me with JOY.

MEMORIAL BENCH

Grief

When my son died, I was not able to cry or express my grief for some time. I was like a zombie frozen in time. Forty days later, at a gathering to honour him, I put my head down on the table and cried in anguish for some time through waves of sensations. Someone came and rubbed my back. I do not know who it was, but I was grateful. I felt relief afterwards, and I thawed out.

Much like constellations, we label the feeling state to identify it, talk about it, and understand it. Like the stars in the universe, we need not know everything about the brain, mind, and body to use the sensations as our guide.

As children grow up, they learn to name their bodily sensations. They discover that certain sensations mean they need to pee, while others mean they need to poop. There are sensations for thirst, hunger, tiredness, sickness, dizziness, and feeling satisfied or full. When they feel sensations of pain, children understand they are physically hurt or sick.

In the same way, children learn to name different constellations of emotions. They discover that certain emotions mean they feel sad, excited, left out, emotionally hurt, emotionally satisfied, prized, disappointed, and angry, among others.

Each feeling state has a behavioural or non-verbal expression. For example:

- Joy is a constellation of pleasant sensations we experience as uplifting and happy. "Jumping for joy" is the behavioural action (or expression) that often accompanies great joy.

- Grief is a constellation of emotionally painful sensations we experience as a loss. Wailing, sobbing, and crying are expressions of grief. Pounding one's body, rocking, and listlessness are behavioural actions that often accompany grief.

FEAR

FEAR

**Nervous-Apprehensive,
A Little Scared**

**Abject Terror,
Blackout**

A Little Worried

Worried Sick

A Little Anxious

**Highly Anxious,
Panic**

Many Shades of Fear

We have learned to label groups of sensations using the Logical Brain. Until children learn the name of certain constellations of sensations, they don't understand what they feel. Even though children are aware they feel something, they don't know what to call it. For example, as we experienced sensations of tears welling up in our eyes and sensations in our throat and chest, we learned to call this constellation of sensations "sadness."

Many of us, particularly children, can't identify what we are feeling; we just know we feel positive/negative/neutral. While we do not need to name or identify a specific emotion to experience or *process* it, most of us like to understand what is happening since we believe/think that we make better decisions when we recognize what is going on.

Same Emotion, Different Names

Different names can be given to some constellations of sensations, yet capture different intensities of the same emotion. "Fearful" has several words or terms that identify the same feeling: apprehensive, nervous, worried, scared, anxious, afraid, panic-stricken, frightened, terrified, and blackout (so terrified that a person dissociates). These names describe different qualities of the same emotion: FEAR.

FEDERER LOSES

Photo by Ben Lewis — Rafael Nadal defeats Roger Federer in the Men's Singles
Final at Australian Tennis Open at Melbourne Park on February 1, 2009

FEDERER WINS

Photo by Frank Molter— Roger Federer wins 20th Grand Slam title at 2018
Australian Open at Melbourne Park

Similar Sensations, Different Feelings

Some feelings are confusing because they appear to be similar. Some sensations between sadness and disappointment are the same, but disappointment has slightly different constellations of sensations. It is possible to be sad and disappointed, or sad and not disappointed, or disappointed and not sad.

Most of the time, we can identify the emotion. "I'm feeling disappointed, not sad," or "I'm feeling disappointed and a little sad," or "I'm not disappointed, just sad."

To access each feeling, we must separate sensations from each constellation. To *process*, we must stay with the sensations of disappointment and breathe through them. The sensations come in waves and gradually dissipate. Next, we must stay with the sensations of sadness and *process* them by breathing through them.

Feeling sad and emotionally "touched" or "moved" have a similar expression—teary, crying, sobbing—yet are opposite in meaning. Sadness is typically unpleasant, while feeling "moved" or "touched" is pleasant. Consider Olympic athletes who win a medal and how they often show emotions that look like those exhibited by someone who has experienced a loss.

The clarity that comes from knowing what we are experiencing is satisfying. Accessing sensations to the depths feels powerful, which is the opposite of feeling powerless. Knowing how to *process* feelings is extremely helpful.

**Jot down some memories
that come to mind.**

Experiencing Many Feelings at Once

It's possible to experience many feelings at once. New parents are often flooded with different feelings. They are excited, happy, and frightened by the enormous responsibility of caring for a child and overwhelmed, concerned, and awed by the tiny new being they have created.

It's also possible to experience opposing feelings simultaneously. Lottery winners often feel excited and discombobulated because their lives have turned upside down. Another example is feeling bittersweet. An hour after putting down my beloved fifteen-year-old cat, I was holding my first newborn grandchild. I felt grief at the loss of my cat and joy with the new baby in my arms.

We can also experience an assortment of jumbled feelings—a cocktail of emotions. We may say we feel "a bit off," "down in the dumps," "on edge," or "jumpy." These are global feelings, and typically, they show a lack of awareness. To understand which ingredients are in the cocktail, we need to access the sensations and sense them for a few seconds or minutes. As we stay with the sensations by being mindful and aware of them, we gather more data from the constellation of each feeling. With the increased sensory data, the feelings differentiate from each other.

When we notice what we are feeling and embrace our sensations, we can experience all the sensations for each emotion. Then we can feel the range of emotions—positive and negative—slight to intense, and feel fully alive and engaged in living our life. Our awareness increases as we access the constellation of sensations for each feeling.

Conflicted

In a session, a client told me that her husband is very worried about her health. He thinks she is working too hard. She said she didn't think so, but she wasn't sure. I had her focus on her inner conflict. I asked her to sit in one chair facing another chair. I directed her to imagine she was having a conversation with herself. She immediately saw her yellow tabby cat, Silke, curled up happily, napping. I asked her to move to the other chair and pretend to be her cat and told her to notice what sensations she felt. As she imagined she was Silke, she laughed and said, "I love to work. I'm like Silke; I can nap and jump up and go to work whenever I want. I know I'm okay, but my husband is worried."

I told her that now that she was clear within herself, she would be clearer with her husband. Then I added, "Maybe he is missing you."

Healthy Appropriate Actions Precipitate from Awareness

If we understand what we are experiencing, we are more likely to take appropriate action if we choose to act. When we fully know ourselves and our circumstances, we are naturally more spontaneous and can trust the steps we may spontaneously take.

Pay attention to your sensations (sensory data includes images, dreams, fantasies, and memories). Much like the stars helped explorers know their position on the planet and guided them on their journeys, your emotions are your guide to how you are at any moment. They may indicate you need to do something, such as take care of yourself, or confirm you are handling things in a way that works or doesn't. They may indicate you need to stop going in one direction and shift to another, or you may get an insight into your situation, which gives you a new perspective that rings true for you.

What's more, when you clearly understand what you are experiencing, you can also interact with others more authentically because you can articulate what you need or how you are feeling. It's difficult to understand or interact with those who are unclear about what they feel. Misinterpretation leads to decisions that create mistaken beliefs, which leads to decisions that take a person in the wrong direction, hurt relationships, or cause problems at work. With clarification on what you are sensing and feeling, you can avoid misunderstandings.

We can be aware of our emotions, feelings, and sensations in our bodies or detach from them.

Let go of
the outcome.

Oh! I've Got to Figure Myself Out First

Bruno is a client of mine who works for a large tech company as a senior engineer. He is divorced from his wife and lives with his partner, Lacy. He has a preteen daughter, and he and Lacy have an 18-month-old toddler.

When COVID-19 hit, he and Lacy were both required to work from home. The pressure of having to stay home exacerbated their relationship issues to the point where Lacy brought up separating. Bruno, who did not want to break up, reached out to me for therapy.

Bruno told me his story. He loves his work; he loves the challenge of solving problems. He said he gets lost in his work and "lives in his head," forgetting about everything, and often works 18-hour days. Lacy works in the HR department at the same company. They no longer have a nanny, and Lacy feels resentful about doing most of the childcare.

Bruno says Lacy keeps wanting something from him, but he does not know what it is.

I explored Bruno's childhood with him. He said his father ruled the family with an iron fist—acting up or acting out were not options. Bruno said he became very good at listening to his father and figuring out what his father wanted and didn't want. However, he did not realize that he had to detach from his body and mind to do so. He learned not to question, try to reason, think for himself, or feel.

Therefore, in all areas of his life, he plays out the same dynamic that he learned in childhood—figure out what others want and need and make that happen. This is why he is good at his job—he figures out what his bosses want and works hard to make it happen, disconnecting from himself in the process.

Similarly, he tries to figure out what his wife wants, but he does not know how to behave in a way that meets her needs.

I worked with Bruno to reconnect with himself. We started by inter-rupting his thinking and doing a scan of his body for sensations. At first, he didn't feel anything; he was numb. However, I was gradually able to bring to his awareness the sensations he was experiencing at the moment. I encouraged and coached him to breathe into whatever sensations he was having. However,

Let things
fall together.

he could only stay with the sensations for a few seconds at a time. Frequently, he would say, "I don't know what I'm supposed to be looking for." I told him to shift from trying to figure it out with logic to sensing the sensations in his body—to be curious about the sensations and to let go of why he was feeling them.

I helped him see that he was doing what his father taught him to do—control the outcome—in all aspects of his life. To do that, he had to detach from his body and mind. I told him to let go of the outcome, which was a new concept for him. He had not realized that he had been trying to control the outcome his entire life.

In ongoing therapy, I helped him focus on his wants, needs, standards, and values. As emotions and feelings came up, I coached him to stay with them and breathe through the sensations. Since he did not have many experiences of emotional closeness, he often got uncomfortable with extended times of intimacy. I advised him not to fight with Lacy when he got uncomfortable but to tell her that he needed a break instead.

As he became more aware of himself, he began to connect with Lacy in mutually satisfactory ways. He finally understood what she wanted from him—connection.

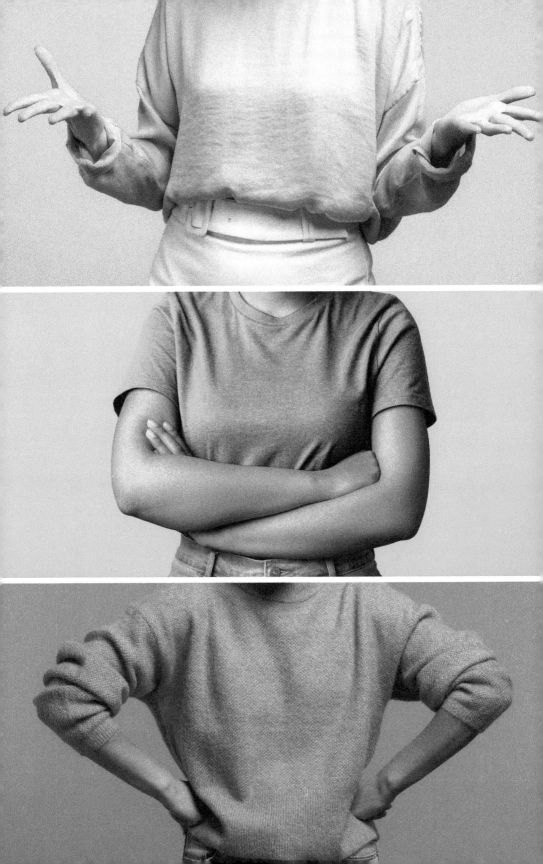

Accessing Emotions

Clients often say to me, "I do not know what I'm feeling." They say this because they are afraid of the sensations and have partially detached from them or can't identify them. Most of us get a twinge—a few sensations from a constellation of a feeling—and quickly shift into the Logical Brain to diagnose the feeling and try to figure out why we are experiencing it.

When clients do this, I guide them from thinking/analyzing to sensing. I tell them to "let go of the need to know." I use a metaphor to explain they need to change how they are handling their feelings. "When you try to figure out what you're feeling with the Logical Brain, it's like trying to enter a house repeatedly through a locked front door without a key. When you access and breathe through the sensations, it's like going through the back door that is unlocked."

In cities, the constellations of stars are harder to see because of the city lights, making it difficult to identify them. However, in the countryside, where there are fewer or no lights, it is much easier to see all the stars that make up each constellation. To see the stars, we need to turn off the lights. In the same way, to know what you feel, you need to "turn off" the Logical Brain and focus on the sensations (images and memories). You pay attention to and get curious about whatever sensations you are aware of by feeling them, experiencing them, and breathing through them.

As you stay with the sensations, you access more of the constellation of whatever emotion you are experiencing. The more sensations you access, the more you feel that emotion, and the more you feel that emotion, the more sensations you access—until you get them all. This gives

you the data you need in a non-verbal form. Once you have more data, you can name it.

"What am I feeling?"

The answer to your question is not in the Logical Brain; it is in your Sensory Brain (limbic system and body).

First, shift to your Sensory Brain by making a statement: I am feeling something. Then, scan your body for sensations, and be curious about the sensations—where are they in your body, are they high/low, strong/weak, blue/or some other colour, are they tight/loose, stringy/spongy? There are no right or wrong sensations. Stay with them and breathe through them.

As you access more and more sensations and breathe through them, your brain will integrate the sensations with the facts (Logical Brain). The answer will be revealed to you. You will intellectually know what you are feeling, and you will experientially know what you are feeling. One type of knowledge confirms the other.

Accessing: "What is, is."

Staying with what you are sensing in the here and now is an effective way to access experiential data. It is a productive way to access what is helpful to know.

Accessing and breathing through the sensations in the here and now is known as *processing*. To analyze the who, what, when, where, why, and how is not relevant or productive at this point. In fact, it gets in the way and impedes accessing/*processing*.

It is essential to know that while becoming clear on a feeling can help us know which action to take or not when it comes to accessing, it doesn't matter what the feeling is or what you call it. If you are experiencing a

Jot down your thoughts.

feeling, it doesn't matter if you are experiencing a different feeling than someone else or whether the feeling you're experiencing is valid or not. When accessing a feeling, it's imperative to remember: "What is, is."

Let's say you are feeling abandoned. Access the sensations of abandonment and breathe through them. As you breathe through the sensations, your brain will synthesize the facts with sensory data, and afterward, you will feel differently—either less bad or a lot better. Later, if you find out you were wrong (you weren't feeling abandoned; you were simply tired), it does not matter. You needed to *process* what you were experiencing at that moment to get to a different accurate psychological place.

Awareness of Self

Without awareness, therapeutic/healthy change is unlikely. Our body is continually sending millions of pieces of information to our brain to make us aware, and our skin is the largest organ in our body. The following exercise will help you connect with the sensations in your body.

Exercise

Awareness Exercise

- Sit down. Turn your attention to your body. Take a breath. The Sensory Brain works more slowly than the Logical Brain.

- Focus on sensations—hot/cold, loose/tight, hard/soft, agitated/calm, etc.

- Start with your feet: wiggle your toes, raise your heels.

- If you are wearing shoes, feel the sensations on your feet, and now, your socks.

- Shift your focus on sensations in your shins, calves, and knees.

- Move up to your lower body. Notice the sensations of your buttocks and your back on the seat.

- Notice any sensations from your genitals, stomach, and intestines.

- Notice the surface you are sitting on—is it soft, hard, wood, cloth?

- Notice the sensations.

- Notice your back—is it leaning against something, or is it free?

- What sensations do you feel in your lower back and upper back?

- Shift to your chest. Notice any sensations in your upper torso, heart, lungs, etc.

- Shift to your neck. What sensations do you feel around your neck? Is it free, or do you have clothing around it?

- Shift to your head, your scalp, and your face—is it tight or relaxed?

- Shift to inside your head. Are there any sensations of aches or pain, excitement, or peacefulness?

- Take a breath.

To become aware, you need to interrupt the Logical Brain thinking and shift to the Sensory Brain sensing.

As you continue to implement these new behaviours, you will increase the time you spend sensing. The more time you spend sensing, the more sensations you will notice and become aware of. The more sensations you get and the more time you spend in the Sensory Brain, the better your brain will synthesize logical data with experiential data, creating new neural pathways. New neural pathways create new ideas, perceptions of circumstances and situations, new sensations, solve problems, etc.

Increase the time you stay with the sensations. With every increase, you will be able to stay in your Sensory Brain, limbic system, and body for increasingly longer times. This is restful and restorative.

I Wish I Had Handled that Differently

When my son was fifteen years old, I made a big mistake when he told me about an early memory he had at the age of four.

He recalled the time we took a family trip to Hawaii, and he was swarmed by red ants on the beach, remembering that he was alone and there was no one around to help him.

His recollection was far from the truth.

I remembered the incident well. We went to Hawaii when he was two and a half years old, not four, and it happened when we were returning from grocery shopping. We had parked the car on the sidewalk, which was covered in sand, near our rental home. We were not on the beach. As my husband and I were unloading the groceries, my son started screaming. We quickly ran to him, my husband lifted him up, and I brushed the red ants off his feet. He was not alone.

When he told me this, I reacted strongly and with intensity. Instead of reflective listening, I needed him to understand that I was a good mom and that we were there for him. He then shut down because I invalidated his experience. I should not have made it about me. Instead, I should have let it be his story and experience, should have forgotten about the facts, and should have just listened. Sometime later, I could have shared my experience of the event with him, not to show him that he was wrong, but to reassure him that I was there for him.

How to Help Others Help Themselves

Helping others *process* their emotions:

When someone is talking to you, let go of thinking whether the facts are accurate. Right now, it does not matter whether the facts are accurate; this is about reflective listening. What matters is their perception of the facts and their experience—the sensations they feel in this moment. Allow them to experience them fully.

Slow down their pace by telling them that what they are saying is important. Tell them how you are impacted by what they are saying, i.e., "I get goosebumps as you tell me that."

Key Takeaways:

- Awareness is knowing what you are experiencing.

- Each emotion has its own constellation of sensations.

- To *process* an emotion, you need to stay with the sensations.

CHAPTER FIVE

Change and Rearrange

"Slow down, you'll get there faster." —Anonymous

Emotions are influenced by perception, and perception influences emotions. This chapter teaches us how the brain makes meaning out of data and how meaning influences emotion.

Meaning often changes when we get more information, reframe information, and when there are changes in sensations.

Making Meaning

Our brain is constantly creating new neural pathways on a small to large scale, working hard to make meaning from every aspect of our lives. This is instinctual, programmed into our DNA from centuries of survival. Typically, this is done on so small a scale that we are not aware of it. People are so focused on making sense out of things that they rarely feel their brains working. I want you to feel your brain working.

Different Ways to Make Meaning

1. Filling in the Gaps

Since we rarely have all the information or data that we need to make meaning, the brain fills in the gaps— sometimes accurately and sometimes inaccurately.

Look at the figure on the left. Notice the sensations in your brain as you look at it.

Feel your brain trying to make meaning out of it and notice how quickly your brain connects the blobs and "sees" the dog. Notice the sensations you experience as you "get it," i.e., make meaning.

This process of filling in the gaps happens all the time, so we rarely notice the physical sensations in our brain as it happens, plus we tend to stay focused on the meaning made in those moments.

I Love That Feeling!

I was learning geometry in Grade 9 and struggling with the theorems. Suddenly, I "got it." The sensations in my head were so intense and satisfying that I remember the moment to this day.

Only when the sensations in our brain are intense enough, do we notice them, like when we have one of those "aha moments." This happens when we suddenly realize something, learn something important, have an idea, or get the gist of a joke. Another metaphor people use to describe this experience is: "It was like a light bulb turned on in my head."

It is difficult to explain this experience in words, so we use the light bulb metaphor to express what happened. When a light bulb goes on, it sheds light on things, enabling us to see/know things we could not see/ know before.

The Brain at Work

When we pay attention, we can feel our brain working and feel it creating new neural pathways.

People believe we all experience life the same way, but we all have a different take on it; we put the data together in different ways based on who we are and our past and current experiences, as well as the sensations we have at the moment, and we then make different meaning out of them.

By American Cartoonist William Ely Hill (1887-1962). The print, titled "My Wife and My Mother-in-Law" was published in *Puck*, an American humour magazine, on November 15, 1915.

What do you see?

If you see a woman, you are right. Is she young or old? If you said "young," you are right. If you said "old," you are right. If you said "both," you are also right.

Even when we are given the same data, we can see different things and make different meaning out it. It is important for us to know that we can all be presented with the same data but make an entirely different meaning from it. If you and I have different takes on an issue and I cannot see the meaning you make and you cannot see the meaning I make, we will have difficulty relating to each other. If we need to resolve something, we may not be able to, or it might be very difficult to resolve. However, if you see what I see and I see what you see, we can relate to each other and connect. Resolving is much easier when we see or "get" both sides of an issue.

Rigid and Flexible Thinking

Flexible thinking occurs when the mind lets go of the meaning made and can see the same data/situation/ circumstances in different ways.

Rigid thinking occurs when the mind locks onto a meaning and cannot let go of it.

Look at the image on the left again. Remember, it is black lines on a white background. If you can only see one woman, i.e., the young woman, try to let go of that image and see whether you can let your mind "see" the old woman. In other words, try to "un-see" what you automatically see. If you cover up part of the image, it may

help you let go of the meaning your mind initially made, enabling you to see the old woman.

Once you see the old woman, look at the whole image again and try to shift back and forth between the two images—old woman and young woman. Notice your brain working to deconstruct the image you saw so easily. This is an ability that can be developed and improved. Working your mind like this is a way to develop flexible thinking. Life is easier with flexible thinking.

The meaning people make out of data is influenced by the experiences they have. We make meaning out of the data we get, whether it is experiential or factual.

Life is like this; even though we all see the same information and have similar experiences, we can also make very different meaning out of what we see, which changes our experiences. This is about the uniqueness of people. The actions we take stem from the meaning we have made about situations or circumstances with which we are presented. We can have different sensations for the same situations. It is possible for the sensations to change. Just like meanings can change, our feelings can change, and our brains can change.

2. Integrating Data

Integration is the result of combining separate things into an integrated whole. When the Logical Brain data is integrated with the Sensory Brain data, they form something completely new, something that did not exist before that can be used in a new way, creating more possibilities. For example, one can wear a sweater but not balls of yarn.

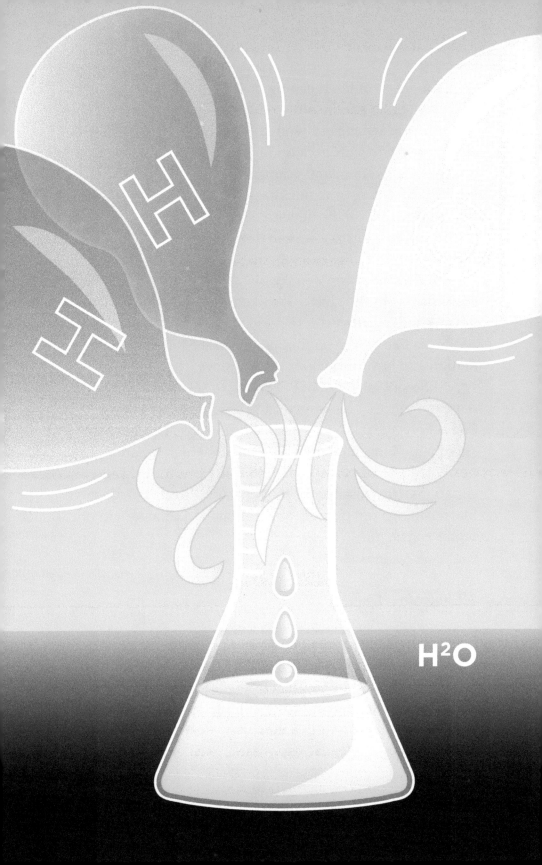

3. Synthesizing Data

Synthesis is the process of two or more entities coming together and forming a new entity, which is entirely different than any of the entities that make it up. The new entity transcends the ones it is made up of because it is in another state.

For example, the caterpillar is perfectly designed to crawl along the ground, trees, and other plants. To become a butterfly, the caterpillar must give up its "way of being" in the world and go into metamorphosis. During metamorphosis, parts of the caterpillar change and come together in a new way to turn into the butterfly. The butterfly has the same DNA but has a new and different way of being in the world. The butterfly's way of being in the world transcends the caterpillar's way of being in the world.

Aha! That's a Different Way to Look at It

Li, a client of mine, told me about her experience when she went for a job interview amid COVID-19.

Li does not wear masks. I don't like to call her an anti-masker, but she is one. She said she has a doctor's note to exempt her from wearing a mask. When setting up the interview, Li checked with the interviewer, and he agreed to the meeting even though she would not be wearing a mask.

She went to the interview. As she entered the building, a man monitoring access to the building stopped her and asked her to put on a mask. She explained that she had a doctor's note exempting her from wearing a mask and produced the note. The monitor told her she would have to leave if she didn't wear a mask. She went on to explain that the person she was meeting agreed to see her without one. Regardless, the man adamantly said, "It does not matter. No mask, no entry!" She had to leave, and she lost her opportunity to interview for the position.

Li told me that she didn't think masks were necessary because there was no evidence they were effective.

I said to her, "Have you noticed how fewer people are getting sick with colds and flu these days?"

She responded, "That's because of COVID-19."

"Exactly," I said. "That proves that masks—and the other things we're doing—are effective."

She had a look of surprise on her face, as though this was new information, but she said nothing.

I went on to say, "It's like fishing for large fish using a small mesh net. You're going to catch a lot of small fish together with the large ones." By reframing the facts, I helped her see the situation in a new way. She had to let go of her view to see it from my perspective.

Changing Meaning

Meaning can change by:

1. Adding More Information—Logical Data/Sensory Data

We rarely have all the information we need to make meaning, yet our brains are continually working to make meaning out of our existence by filling in the gaps. When we get more information, that is, more data—logical and/ or sensory—the meaning often changes.

2. Changing the Context

Reframe the same information in a new way. Reframing means to frame or express information—words, concepts, plans— differently.

To reframe, you need to deconstruct the current meaning and reconstruct a new/different meaning.

Death / Rebirth

My client, Mandeep, had a sister who died before Christmas 2019. Mandeep
had been struggling with the loss because she was estranged from everyone in
her family. She said that she and her sister did not get along when growing up
but had reconnected as adults, making her feel less alone in the world. When
her sister unexpectedly died, Mandeep felt alone again. She was so distraught
that she could not work, so she went on medical leave. Not too long after that,
COVID-19 hit and because of her grief, compounded with the lockdown, she
quit her job.

Mandeep turned to an aunt who had been good to her but felt her aunt's
support was surface-level at best.

So, Mandeep reached out for therapy and was referred to me. Because she
lived in Europe, we connected via videoconferencing.

I listened to Mandeep's story. She grew up in a family in which she
felt invisible. From her experiences as a child, she developed a belief about
herself—I don't matter; I only matter if I am pleasing others. She was always
focused on others, not herself, trying to figure out what others wanted/needed
and making it happen.

I told her that she had what I call a mistaken belief, and I told her it was
not true.

I then worked with her to change this belief. I developed a small ritual to
deconstruct the belief and then asked her to create her own belief. This started
to shift how she felt about herself.

In therapy, I facilitated her expressing and processing her grief at the loss
of her sister, her sense of abandonment, and utter aloneness in the world. I
shared with her my story of loss and how it impacted me, which connected us.
I sent her a bead bracelet to remind her to take a breath when she noticed it
and to feel somewhat connected to me—half-way around the globe.

Her grief was deep and had gone on for a long time. She had disturbing
dreams. I shared with her my experience of the time I died in a dream. I told
her that dying in a dream can mean letting go of a part of yourself that you

*need to let go of—a part of you that you were not born with but helped you
survive childhood.*

About a month later, I received the following email from Mandeep:

"I had a strange dream last night. I am a terrible sleeper and hardly
dream. In it, my sister died, but then shortly after, my aunt and Gregory
(her life coach) also died. The dream felt very sad, but it made me think of the
dream you said you had about dying. I have been trying to do a lot of work on
getting in tune with what I want rather than what other people have told me
I want. I am beginning to explore career paths that once seemed crazy to me.
I'm curious if the two are related. Maybe it signifies that I'm ready to step into
my own."

I was pleased that she had taken in the information about death and dying
in dreams. It helped her frame her experience in an emotionally healthy way,
which she would not have been able to do without this information.

I told her that the dream was positive. Death is about letting go, and
her dream meant she was letting go of the significant people in her life. With
Gregory, it meant she was letting go of him too because she no longer needed
him in the same way. I told her that she had let go of needing others because
she had reclaimed the young child within who was frozen in time.

She had created new neural pathways and was ready to start focusing on
her life and passions.

3. Shifting Sensations

Our senses are constantly picking up data from the universe and sending it to our brains, whether we are awake/asleep, focused on a task or lounging on the swing on the back porch. Most of the time, we are not aware of this accumulation of information. When we sleep, our brain goes into REM sleep, and all the data integrates and synthesizes it with what our Logical Brain has thought about, analyzed, and learned. Frequently, we get sensations that build up and break into our awareness.

Examples of shifting sensations:

The Relationship Ran Its Course

Tyrell, born in Trinidad, has lived in Canada for 21 years. He met his wife, Elizabeth, years ago when she was vacationing in Trinidad. He came from a large, low-income family. He and Elizabeth fell in love, and two years later, they were married and living in Canada. They both wanted a family and happily agreed that she would be the breadwinner and he would stay home with the children. This arrangement worked well for many years.

When their children were in elementary school, things shifted, and Tyrell started dabbling in real estate. However, he did not find much success in real estate but had always been passionate about music. Unfortunately, it was not lucrative, so he continued to ride Elizabeth's coattails throughout the marriage.

When their children reached their teenage years, their marriage went into a natural stage of reorganization. Since both Tyrell and Elizabeth realized that their children would leave home in a few years, they did what most couples do at this stage; they reassessed their spousal relationship.

So, Tyrell and Elizabeth came to therapy, and we identified their negative interactive cycle. Elizabeth was tired of doing the emotional and financial heavy-lifting, and Tyrell was tired of being the nanny and running the household. They still cared about each other, so they made satisfactory adjustments.

And then COVID-19 happened, and their relationship went into crisis mode. The pressure and tension from lockdown tipped their coping over the edge. Spending so much time together blew open the cracks in their marriage. There was little goodwill left between them and even less love, and the resentment was palpable between them.

They decided to have a trial separation. Even though Tyrell did not have a stable, adequate income, he decided it was in his and their children's best interests to move out. It was time for him to come into his own as an adult, man, and individual in his own right. He was apprehensive yet accepting of this personal growth.

Figure yourself out here.

The rest of their sessions focused on grieving the breakup of their family unit. I helped each process their emotions by guiding them to breathe through the sensations of grief and loss to the depths. As the intensity of the sensations lessened, each started to feel a sense of relief.

I told them that a trial separation is just that—a trial. Sometimes, couples need to completely let go of the way each had been in the marriage before there is any possibility of reconnecting in a new way. I told them that their old marriage was dead and that it needed to die. It was not working for either one of them, and it was no longer emotionally healthy for their children. I encouraged each to let the old marriage die without guilt or judgment—to shift sensations. I talked to them about the concept of death/rebirth. I told them that if they can come together again in the future in a new way, they will create a new marriage that will likely last the rest of their lives.

I told them that a trial separation is just that—a trial. Sometimes, couples need to completely let go of the way each had been in the marriage before there is any possibility of reconnecting in a new way. I told them that their old marriage was dead and that it needed to die. It was not working for either one of them, and it was no longer emotionally healthy for their children. I encouraged each to let the old marriage die without guilt or judgment—to shift sensations. I talked to them about the concept of death/rebirth. I told them that if they can come together again in the future in a new way, they will create a new marriage that will likely last the rest of their lives.

Emotionally Frozen

Macklem, a 58-year-old married man, was referred to me by his doctor. He was deeply depressed, so depressed that he could barely talk.

Prior to his first marriage, he had been in a long-term relationship for 25 years with a woman 18 years his senior. Three years ago, he was blindsided by his common-law partner's sudden ending of the relationship. He did not see it coming and was devastated. He described himself as "a ship that had lost anchor in the night and was being washed up on the rocks."

He immediately went online, quickly met a woman, and married her shortly afterwards. Now, three years later, he is deeply depressed. He describes his current wife as "very nice and kind" and says he's been floating through their marriage the past three years.

Then COVID-19 hit.

Macklem is a writer and usually works from home. Before COVID-19, his wife worked at her office. With both forced to work from home, the emptiness of their relationship became palpable.

Macklem was terrified of the relationship ending because he feared the sensations he experienced with his previous breakup. However, he didn't articulate it that way; he said he was terrified of being "left to float again." Once he started therapy, he felt relief at being able to tell someone his story.

I advised him not to make any decisions about his current relationship; his focus needed to be on his personal recovery.

I asked him to tell me about his childhood, and he told me that his father was always angry and that his parents fought a lot. One memory stood out for him: He was 13-years-old and wanted to attend a concert with his friends. However, his father wouldn't let him, stating he was too young. Regardless, he snuck out and went with his friends anyway. When his father found out, he beat him badly, and it took him a long time to recover from the physical and emotional trauma.

I talked to him about how important puberty is and how a father's developmental task is to welcome their sons into manhood. I told him his father did *the opposite. The beating traumatized him, leaving him frozen in time at age 13 (probably even younger). He resonated strongly with what I said.*

I told him that our therapeutic work needed to revolve around helping him access and process the old wound and heal from it—he had been living in limbo because he was no longer a child yet had not come into his own as an adult, male, and individual in his own right.

I also told him how he had no one who advocated for him throughout his life, so he could not learn to advocate for himself.

In therapy, I helped him facilitate his accessing and expressing the sensations of terror and alienation at being left afloat.

I typically give clients homeplay (not homework) to do between sessions. I suggested to him that he start taking classes in some attacking-type sport, such as boxing, wrestling, martial arts, etc., to get the skills to fight for himself and revise his mistaken belief to understand that he was worthy and worth fighting for.

He chose boxing and started feeling better about himself almost immediately, and it showed in the way he carried himself.

Macklem is still in his relationship; it is changing because he is changing. I advised him to let go of the outcome; time will tell if he and his wife can develop a new relationship or let go of this one because it has run its course. It will be his decision from a healed place.

Modus Operandi

Modus operandi is a consistent way/pattern of operating in life with the self, others, and the world in general. It is a person's "way of being" in the world. It begins at birth and is stabilized around five to six years of life. It may stay the same for a person's lifetime or be changed by the circumstances and conditions of a person's environment. It can also be changed by focusing on the modus operandi directly.

Babies are born with innate characteristics that stem from their genetics, energy levels (passive/active, fragility/hardiness), levels of curiosity, sensitivities, interests, urges, and the need to attach. We tend to think of babies as all the same. In many ways, they are. However, from birth, they adapt these characteristics to meet their survival needs. Each baby is different in significant ways. How the mother (and other caregivers) interacts with the child impacts the child's emotional and physical development. What the child witnesses also impacts their emotional and physical development.

From birth to age six, babies and children must figure out their bodies and how they work. They must figure out how to interact with others to best survive in their family, culture, and the world. Most of what they learn is by mimicking others, by interacting with others (teaching, helping, guiding), and trial and error. Children tend to do more of what gives them pleasurable feelings/sensations and avoid what gives them unpleasant feelings/sensations.

By age seven, children have had millions of experiences. From all those experiences, they have figured out patterns and recurring events and adapted to them. Eventually, they developed an idiosyncratic (unique) "way of being" for living their lives. They have a sense of

Bea's Modus Operandi

When I was 36, my marriage went into a natural reorganization when my youngest child entered kindergarten. For seven years, my life had been focused on raising my babies and caring for our home. Our marriage needed to shift, and we needed to make changes, but we were not handling it well. I found a therapist, and in talking with the therapist, I discovered my modus operandi.

I lived on a farm which was often dangerous. I was the youngest of four in my family. My parents were hard-working. My siblings often had to look after me while mom and dad worked. They were bigger, older, and more capable than I was.

I am...little and helpless. (I was emotionally developmentally arrested at an infant level)

Others are...smarter, more competent, more capable than.

The world is...a dangerous place.

So therefore...I must always have someone to look after me.

Here I was at 36, acting like a little girl. I was certainly not little and helpless. I was successfully running a household and mothering two children. The world was a dangerous place, but it was certainly not THAT dangerous. I did not need anyone to look after me, including my husband. However, I wanted a healthy grown-up relationship with him.

Therapy focused on helping me process the trauma I experienced in childhood.

who they are, who others are, and how the world is. From this, they conclude how to be or not be, what to do or not do to best survive, cope, and thrive. At this young age, they are inexperienced and ignorant of many factors. The conclusions they make may be accurate, partially accurate, or they may not be accurate at all. Often, they are not.

Humans tend to behave in ways that bring sensations of pleasure and satisfaction and are meaningful to them. They want to feel sensations of safety and security. They tend to behave in ways to avoid sensations that cause discomfort and pain and are meaningless. Most people do not want to feel sensations of risk, danger, and insecurity.

Associations influence meaning. Many people go about their everyday lives unaware that they are avoiding sensations. People develop habits to avoid situations, circumstances, and people they associate with stressful and uncomfortable sensations they have felt in the past. Their intent is to manifest sensations that they like and enjoy.

However, people will also stay in situations they associate with danger because they are familiar and give the illusion of safety. For example, people will stay in abusive relationships because they occasionally experience moments of love and safety amongst the chaos and danger.

Children need to make sense of the world to survive. By the age of seven, children have created a modus operandi. They have made meaning out of their lives. This is how they operate in the world. They need to know they developed this mode, and it can be changed. Most people are convinced they are genetically programmed and they cannot be changed. It's an adaptation to the world (family, culture, geographically / economically) they are born into.

Depending on the events and circumstances, a person's modus operandi can be changed, but often, it is not because people do not think they can change and

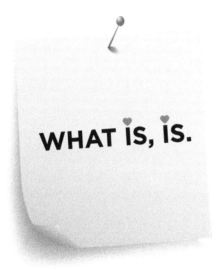

because they don't know how to change. A person's modus operandi may work well in childhood, but it does not work well in adulthood. While it may help us survive when we are children by serving as a coping mechanism, it can often keep us from thriving as adults.

A person's modus operandi becomes a pattern of their entrenched habits. Fortunately, habits can be changed. Even bad habits, such as drinking and smoking, can be changed. Therefore, a person's modus operandi can be changed. We can identify the strengths of our modus operandi and build on them, and we can identify the weaknesses, target them, and change them. People often say, "This is who I am" (stubborn, lazy, hard, etc.) as though they were born that way. Typically, they were not.

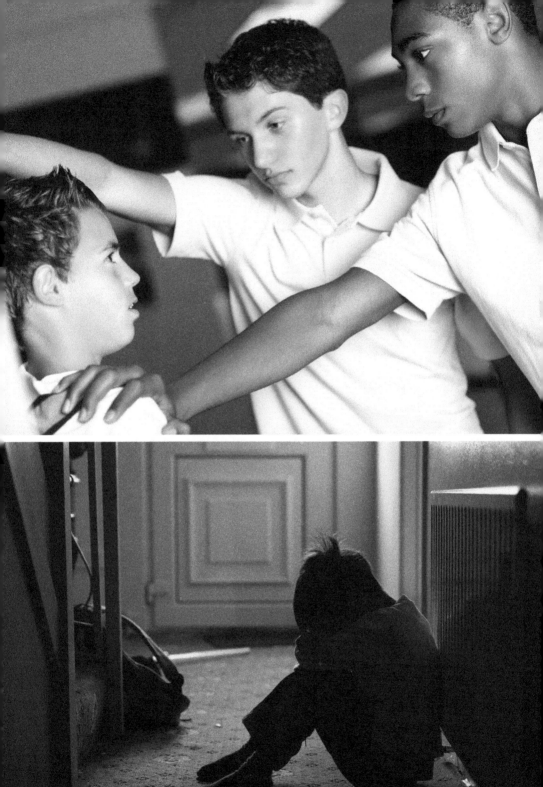

Transcending the Old Way

Gusto and Francesca had been seeing me for couple's counselling before COVID. At first, the constant togetherness of lockdown alleviated issues as they were alone together most of the time. But as the lockdown continued and the tension between them intensified, Francesca, a runner, started going for longer runs. They returned for couples counselling.

Gusto was a large man whose mother abandoned him when he was five years old. Francesca was a petit woman who grew up with a father who beat her frequently. Each had not felt safe in their family of origin for different reasons.

In therapy, we identified the negative interactive pattern between them. Gusto would often get insecure when his wife would go out with her friends. His modus operandi was to avoid feelings of abandonment. Often, she would be gone for 3-4 hours at a time when she went for a run. When Gusto felt the sensations of abandonment, he would cling to Francesca when she left or when she returned.

Francesca feared being dominated and controlled. Her modus operandi was to avoid being dominated. When Gusto clung to her, she would feel the sensations of being trapped, and she would pull away. When she pulled away, Gusto's abandonment issues would get triggered, and he would cling to her more. The more he would cling to her, the more controlled she would feel. They played this dynamic out in every aspect of their lives.

I worked with Gusto on processing his painful sensations of abandonment. I helped him access and breathe through the waves of intense sensations. When he was triggered, the sensations were so distressing that he would get desperate and believe that only hanging onto Francesca would stop them. He knew that this triggered her fear of being dominated, but he could not stop himself.

Similarly, I worked with Francesca to process the sensations of feeling trapped and dominated. I facilitated her breathing through the sensations and staying with them instead of trying to stop them. When she felt dominated,

the sensations were so awful and intense that she just wanted them to stop, and she had to get away

Several weeks later, they returned. They looked different and sounded different. They had a sense of calm within themselves and with each other. They had transcended the old dynamic.

They told me that they got into a physical altercation that escalated about a week after our last session. Gusto had pinned Francesca down, with his big hands gripping her wrists. He knew if he let her go, she would run out of the home, and his heart would break. Francesca was fighting for her life. She thought for sure she was going to die.

Then something happened. They do not know who did what first, but Gusto eased his grip seemingly at the same time as Francesca struggled less. At that moment, each felt loved and safe. Gusto said he knew that Francesca was fighting for her life, but the fact that she lessened her struggle meant she loved him. Similarly, Francesca said she knew Gusto was terrified she would abandon him forever, so when he loosened his grip on her wrists, she felt loved and safe. This shattered the tension between them, and they wrapped their arms around each other and cried with joy and relief.

They have a new relationship with each other that has a calm peace at the core.

Now when Francesca goes out, Gusto is not triggered, so he does not cling to her. When she comes back, she is loving and affectionate. She engages in more vigorous lovemaking because she is not afraid anymore, which Gusto loves because it reinforces his sense of connection with her.

Exercise

Identify your modus operandi by exploring your memories.

- They may be happy, fun, funny, and/or they may be sad, painful, scary.

- Take each one by itself and relive it as best you can.

- The memory is stored in the Sensory Brain, so allow yourself the time to access it.

- As you recall it, be aware of any sensations that are evoked.

- Breathe through the sensations.

- If you find a memory to be traumatic during this process, you might want to explore it with a professional. You may be recreating the trauma in your current life if it is not healed.

How to Help Others Help Themselves

Share your memories and dreams with others. However, choose wisely with whom to share them as you are sharing your unconscious way of operating in the world.

Key Takeaways:

- Emotions impact meaning and meaning impacts emotions.

- Meaning is in the eye of the beholder and can change.

- Modus operandi is a person's "way of being" in the world.

- A person's modus operandi can change.

CHAPTER SIX

High Stakes, Opportunity for Change

"In Chinese, the word for 'crisis' also bears the meaning of opportunity." —Anonymous

Connection Is the Antidote to Alienation

Throughout history, there have been catastrophes and disasters: fires, floods, earthquakes, tornadoes, hurricanes, etc. What typically happens is that people come together to help each other. They sandbag in floods, clean up messes, rebuild homes, prepare food for those working, collect clothing, goods, and other essentials that people who have lost everything need, etc. They grieve with each other around lost loved ones, lost homes, and loss of assets. They hug and provide physical comfort. In this collective activity, they bond with each other, often making new friends and business associates for life. Plus, they do not feel alone in the world. They feel a togetherness, which feels safe and helps them survive.

*Change is more
likely when the stakes
are high.*

Bonding Through Disaster

When I was little, we moved from the farm to a nearby town—Portage la Prairie was only 16 miles from our farm, so my father would commute. We lived about 50 miles from the central city, Winnipeg, situated on two rivers— the Red River and the Assiniboine River. Some winters, we would get lots of snow, none of which would melt until spring. I was six when we had one of those winters. When spring came that year, both rivers overflowed. People and families had to be evacuated. I guess there was not enough room in Winnipeg, so many families were brought to our town.

Our house was surrounded by churches—the Catholic one just half a block away from the intersection facing our home, the Baptist one kitty-corner from us, the United Church behind us and one street over, and the Presbyterian one only six doors down.

All the churches opened their basements and empty rooms for displaced families during the flood. I remember my neighbourhood being very busy with all the new people around. However, despite being crammed into these churches, I remember the displaced families would sing, shovel the snow, cook, and go for walks together. Even though they were experiencing hardship, they were also having a good time. There was a lot of handshaking, clapping each other on the back, laughter, and jokes. I'm sure there was pain, fear, and discomfort, but I did not see it. Instead, I witnessed the connections.

What struck me at age six was how people came together and helped each other and how people from different religions got along.

I didn't think much of it when I was a child, but in hindsight, I can see that people bonded with each other and connected to each other. The flood forced them into a new situation, and they struggled, but they also made long-term friends and were left with many stories to tell.

The current global pandemic is very different. We are forced to stay apart; we cannot gather in families unless we live in the same home; we cannot gather in groups or even in threes. We are required to self-isolate as much as possible. We cannot invite people to our homes; we cannot get together in restaurants or pubs to share food and drink; we cannot gather in groups to support and commiserate with each other. We cannot hug and kiss!

At least, families have each other. However, many of us (and I am one) live alone. Yes, we have the internet, email, photos, videos, video games, and movies to entertain us, which certainly helps. However, it is much more difficult to connect and bond online than in person.

I certainly do not want to be responsible for picking up the virus from someone or something and infecting myself, and becoming a burden to my children. I also don't want to put my children and grandchild at risk, so I'm staying at home as much as possible. When I do go out, I take precautions.

This is a lonely global disaster. It is disconnecting us from each other and making supporting each other more difficult. It is the opposite of bonding; it is alienating.

This type of disaster is Mother Nature's way of giving us a reality check. We were all in a bubble, humming along and feeling mostly in control of our lives. We were colluding with each other that this is normal. However, the control we experienced was an illusion. Mother Nature came along with her super virus and popped the bubble! Now we know how little control we had then and have now.

It is terrifying to think that we, in fact, have no control, that we are powerless to influence our circumstances. If so, we cannot count on anything lasting or staying the same over time. How do we go about living our lives? What, if anything, do we have control over or can we influence?

Our Relationship with Ourselves

What we can control is our relationship with ourselves. We can understand our bodies and our brains and learn how they function at their best. We can stop *managing* our emotions and start *processing* them instead. We can let go of the outcome and live our lives more fully and with more aliveness. We can stay connected to ourselves and ground ourselves in our bodies and our senses. Or, we can disconnect from our bodies and live in our heads, dealing with the endless chatter about how to live or not live our lives.

If we mistreat, bully, disparage, harshly criticize, and shame and blame ourselves, our personal energy is opposed and pitted against the self. We may have a lot of energy, but it is busy and not available. Instead, we experience more emotional and physical pain, our self-esteem goes down, decision-making becomes more difficult, our creativity is compromised, and we have a much harder time handling life. There is little or no goodwill, so getting along with others is also more difficult. More symptoms such as depression, sadness, fear, panic, anxiety, aloneness, and powerlessness also become heightened. These sensations are so unbearable that we shift into anger to get respite from them.

The Function and Purpose of Anger

In turbulent times, life is unpredictable. Every day brings news—some good but mostly bad. The virus is still spreading; people are still dying. As I write this page, most of the world is still in lockdown. Most stores are still closed. If any restaurants are open, it's only for take-out. There is nowhere to go except outside, and we must keep our distance from others. Even parks, playgrounds, beaches, playing fields, tracks, and gyms are still off-limits. There is no place where we can gather together. Tension builds.

If there is no way to release the tension, people often get irritable, angry, and intolerant with each other.

Stack of Coins

Mary sighed. She'd blown her top—again. After the last time, she'd promised herself that she would not do it anymore, but she'd just lost it again.

Mary had been cleaning the home for a couple of hours. Ralph had come home from soccer and was in the shower. She walked into the bedroom to get something and found a pile of his sweaty clothes on the floor. This was an ongoing struggle between them. Mary had asked him many times to put his dirty clothes in the clothes hamper. Annoyed, Mary swept up the clothes, put them away, and went back to cleaning the home. Half an hour later, she walked into the bathroom and saw his wet towel lying on the bathroom floor. She lost it and went into a rage. She grabbed the towel and stomped off to find him. He was sitting on the patio, relaxing. Seeing him relaxed infuriated her even more. She threw the towel in his face and yelled obscenities at him. Finally, she stomped off. Ralph sat there in shock, wondering what had just happened: "It was just a towel."

Often there is a cycle of anger and peace. A person blows-up, and then there is a period of peace. But life is life. Things happen, and often, they are not significant. A small annoying event will happen, and it will get dismissed. There is tension. Another irritating event follows, and it gets pushed under the rug. Tension increases. Another frustrating event and anger is pushed aside. More tension. After several more frustrating events, another small event happens, and a person blows up in rage. Usually, there is confusion because the nature of the event did not warrant the intensity of the anger. Others will ask, "How could you get so mad about that?" However, the tension is released. Now there is peace again—at least for a while. *Anger has a function.*

Anger is typically a secondary feeling. When people shift into anger, the sensations of anger disguise the sensations of vulnerability. The sensations of vulnerability do not go away; they go into the background. Feeling angry is better than feeling the sensations of humiliation, rejection, or any other vulnerable feeling. When people feel angry, they feel sensations of power, not vulnerability. With anger, it may be possible to change what is going on for better or worse. *Anger has a purpose.*

Vicarious Ambition

James watched as his son, a talented goalie, let in a goal that lost the game. Exasperated, he let out a cry of disgust. After the game, James berated his son for not trying hard enough. His discouraged son tried to convince his father that he had tried as hard as he could. Both felt bad.

James lived vicariously through his son. When his son did well, James felt proud and important. When his son did not do well, James felt like a failure. James hated the sensations of failure, so he shifted into anger and got on his son's case.

When people get angry, they are looking for a specific outcome. James needed his son to do well so that he could feel good about himself. He got angry at his son, pressuring him into trying harder. Most children feel uncomfortable when their parents are angry, so they try to do whatever it is that will stop the anger, whether it is good for them or not. They become more focused on what their parents are feeling than on the activity, making it harder for them to do well.

So, Where Do We Start? What Do We Do?

First, start with yourself.

Start by focusing on your anger and *processing* it. By *processing* your anger, it brings you to the underlying vulnerability fueling your anger. Using the new strategy of shifting from the Logical Brain and into the Sensory Brain, stay focused on the sensations and breathe through them until all the waves have gone. Practice this until it becomes your new habit.

Your anger will shift and change in healthy ways, not by reasoning, reframing, or logic, but from a synthesis of your Logical Brain data with your Sensory Brain data to form new neural pathways, that is, new connections that you did not have before. The new neural pathways have new/different sensations.

Your emotions and how you handle and *process* them impact all your relationships. By now, you know that when you *process* your emotions, your personal energy is aligned and available to you to handle whatever life throws your way. A positive ripple effect occurs with all you encounter.

When you take care of your emotions in a healthy and responsible way, your relationships with others will improve and be easier—even "less bad" is an improvement.

The one who
teaches learns
the most.

Next, teach someone else.

When someone is fearful, acknowledge their fear—whether real or imagined—and help them *process* the fear.

When parents are distressed, their children become distressed. Children intuitively know that they need their parents to be okay and function well for them to best survive. Children will turn themselves inside out trying to reassure, help, and be okay so that their parents will be okay. Children will lie, cheat, deny their own feelings, get sick, etc., if it helps their parents be okay.

Children need to be attached (connected) to their caregivers, whoever they may be. Children who are attached survive better than children who are not attached. Again, this connection is critical for survival.

Children whose parents attach securely to their children and allow/encourage them to attach securely to them (the parents) do better in life than children whose parents are ambivalent about attachment or reject attachment. Attachment patterns are passed down from one generation to the next. Children learn how to connect from parents and caregivers, and they, in turn, teach the next generation. Our attachment history plays a crucial role in determining how we relate in adult romantic relationships and how we relate to our children. However, it is not what happened to us as children that matters most—it is how we deal with it.

Generalized Anxiety

After months of living through COVID-19, Amber came to see me for therapy. She told me that over the past several months, her daughter had started to eat very little, looked exhausted, and was very quiet and subdued. One evening, she took her daughter for a walk with their dog and started a conversation with her. Amber told me that she let her daughter know that she noticed she wasn't her usual self. She then asked her daughter if there was something she wanted to talk about.

Her daughter started to cry and said there was a rumour going around school that the school would close and she would have to complete her schooling online. Her daughter is a very social child, so this news was even harder for her to digest. Amber told me that she talked to her daughter about the different aspects of what could happen if that was the case. For example, she told her that she would help her navigate online schooling as she understood it could be difficult at first and told her that although she wouldn't be able to see her friends in person, they could make arrangements to see them virtually. She also told her that they would continue to spend time together as a family, playing games and doing things together so that they would stay connected. She reassured her that they would take it one step at a time and deal with it as it came together.

Amber told me that her daughter then hugged her, thanking her for taking the time to speak to her and told her that she felt much better. Her daughter said that many of her friends had mentioned being worried about it, and when they tried to discuss it with their parents, their parents would tell them not to worry about it; there was nothing they could do but deal with it.

I was impressed with how Amber handled the situation, and at the end of the session, I applauded her parenting.

The best ways parents can help their children are:

- learn how to *process* their own emotions and model *processing* of their emotions.

- model how to live an emotionally healthy way of being in the world.

- validate their child's experiences and emotions.

They can do this by:

- modelling age-appropriate *processing* of emotions (i.e., parents do not burden their children with adult emotions/problems).

- providing emotional and sometimes physical containers for children until they can be their own container.

- teaching their children how to *process* their emotions.

Things to avoid doing or saying:

- "There's nothing to be afraid of." This invalidates the child's feelings. It does not matter if their fear is rational or irrational; they are experiencing fear in some form.

- "Go play with the dog," or "Go play your video games." This dismisses the child's feelings.

- "Don't bother me right now. I'm busy." This disconnects the parent from the child.

- "There's nothing wrong. Don't worry." Lying to the child creates distrust. Your words and body language do not match, and, therefore, this creates confusion for the child.

Channel
your anger
constructively.

Anger Disconnects People from Themselves and Each Other

Anger is a powerful energy. It can be used for good. For example, an exasperated lover shaking his lover's shoulders, saying, "What do I have to do to convince you that I love you?" The anger here may or may not be experienced as "loving," but often, the intensity of the lover's expression, both verbally and non-verbally, may get through their partner's self-protecting emotional wall, that is, the lover experiences a letting go and a receiving of their partner's genuine love.

In childhood, the quality of family life has a significant physical and emotional impact on babies and toddlers as they are incredibly vulnerable and powerless. Lucky are the babies who have loving parents that welcome them into the family and are cradled in peace, love, and safety. They are immediately shown positive modelling of how to interact with those we love.

In families like these, anger is expressed and used in healthy ways. Anger tends to be used appropriately in terms of "the punishment fits the crime," meaning the size and severity of the discipline fits the extent and seriousness of the infraction.

Tabled Anger

Sam pulled into her garage after a long hectic day at work. As she got out of her car, she heard glass breaking. She went around the corner of her home and saw the shattered living room window. Her son and his friends stood on the street frozen. One of the boys had hit the baseball through the window. Sam was enraged! Last time it was the neighbour's bedroom window. She had told them many times to practice in the schoolyard nearby. She wanted to scream at them and slap them silly!

Sam knew that she was too angry to deal with the boys right then and told them so. She sent her son to his room and sent his friends home. She changed into her jeans and a T-shirt, went out into the backyard, and chopped some wood. As she chopped, her rage dissipated. She was still angry but not enraged. Then she got her son to help her put some plywood over the broken window. Later that evening, she and her husband sat down with their son to deal with the problem.

Let the page speak to you.

Express yourself.

Parents set the tone for the family atmosphere. When parents are connected, children feel safe; they see how their parents connect, thus modelling how to connect. Just as children learn a language, they learn by witnessing and experiencing family interactions.

Even families who struggle financially can be rich in family dynamics.

Children who grow up feeling loved, valued, and have a sense of belonging are connected to themselves. They are born connected and stay connected, and they find it easy to connect with others, especially like-minded people.

Then there are the children who are not so lucky. They may be fortunate in some ways, but not in others. In Tim Crother's *Queen of Katwe* (true story), Phiona is born into extreme poverty to an illiterate mother who had several children from different fathers. Phiona's father abandoned the family, and her family struggled to stay alive every day. Phiona's mother would cook some corn and would send five-year-old Phiona into the streets to sell it. On some days, Phiona would come back with a few coins, but she was often attacked by older starving children who bullied her and stole the corn and any coins she might have had.

In circumstances like these, children need to disconnect from their bodies to survive. They need to numb the sensations of hunger, the sensations of terror when they feel unsafe, the discomfort of old, torn, dirty clothing, etc. The struggle to survive often makes people hard because their need for survival depends on it. They cannot care about what happens to others, or they won't survive. Therefore, it is too dangerous to connect to others. Also, children who are tired, hungry, and don't feel they belong are often mean to others because they are powerless, and being mean gives them some sensations of power.

Children born into difficult circumstances "turn off' their senses; they do not see, hear, taste, touch, or smell in a natural way—it's too painful, hurtful, ugly, noisy, disgusting, and distasteful, and it makes them too vulnerable.

In circumstances like these, anger helps to mask unpleasant sensations. As feeling numb is okay in the short term, it makes one feel inhuman in the long term. Anger has sensations that give respite to the humanoid quality of daily life.

Anger creates distance. Often family members do not want to be close to each other emotionally or physically, but they don't necessarily say so. Instead, they get angry, and others naturally pull away.

For babies, toddlers, and even older children, adults are giants who are in control of their lives in every way. When parents get angry, children get frightened, often so frightened they freeze both emotionally and physically.

In times of a pandemic, particularly this pandemic, it is as if the world has turned upside down and little or nothing is the same—someone has thrown out the rule book for living.

How to Deepen Connections

Small acts of connection can be powerful. When you walk along the street, do you look at people? Do you smile at them? Do you acknowledge them with your eyes? Do you speak to them? Do you connect with them? Do they exist to you as human beings like yourself? Or, are they objects, things to step around and not bump into?

When you walk along the street, do people look at you? Do they smile at you? Do they acknowledge you with their eyes? Do they speak to you? Do they connect with you? Do you feel you exist to them as a fellow human being? Or, do you feel like an object to them, a thing to step around and not bump into?

Couples who are connected demonstrate it in many small ways. At a gathering, the connected couple is not joined at the hip; they circulate and interact with other guests and occasionally make eye contact with each other from across the room. They will come by to check in with their partner, then move on again. These small interactions are not done in a controlling or manipulative manner; they are mutually satisfying. They convey that they matter to each other.

What if . . .

. . . we started to connect more in small ways? It does not matter who the person is. It could be a lover, parent, child, relative, neighbour, acquaintance, supermarket clerk, etc.

. . . we smiled more at children—at our own and at total strangers' children? Just eye contact and a smile. Nothing more. No agenda. Just acknowledgement that they exist.

. . . we learned the server's name when we eat at a restaurant? Connection with respect.

. . . we expressed appreciation more often. "I appreciate you helping me out last night/week/month."

How would that be for you? What difference would it make to your life? When you don't know what to do, experiment and see what happens!

When children feel connected to family members, they thrive. A few minutes of connection a day can make all the difference to a child and their parents.

This time is an amazing and unusual opportunity for parents to connect with their children and vice versa. When adults play, children feel connected to them.

So, what can we do?

1. Create pockets of hope for yourself and your family:

   - Carve out a few minutes every day to play together. Set a timer.

   - Turn all technology off for an agreed-upon time.

   - Put the rest of the world on hold for thirty minutes and have fun together.

   - Engage fully during the agreed-upon time.

2. Brainstorm ideas and involve your children as much as possible so that they will engage more in the process:

   - Sing/play music together.

   - Belly laugh.

   - Have a dance party. How many different dances can you learn?

3. Play active games:

   - Darts

   - Badminton

   - Basketball

   - Hopscotch

   - Make up your own game

Let your ideas flow!

4. Have a mock fight. This helps to dispel the tension in the group/family:

    - Pillow fight

    - Beanbag fight

    - Water balloon fight

    - Noodle fight

Note: even just suggesting having a fight often dispels tension.

5. Suggest fun challenges:

    - Who can create the goofiest game?

    - Make the goofiest face?

    - Dance the goofiest dance, etc.?

6. Create moments of peace, joy, and fun (15–30 minutes)

    - Create your own time warp in which you pretend everything is okay and enjoy it. It's not much, but it gives some respite from the black cloud hanging over us all.

It's hard for children to see their parents worried, fearful, and sad all the time. When parents create these bubbles of peace and fun, it gives their children hope. At the same time, parents get pleasure from giving their children small pockets of peace and joy.

The power of connection—it is bonding.

Exercise

When people are angry, they want to attack or defend—anger has a purpose—to make something happen or stop something from happening.

When you are angry, there are many ways to constructively and productively express your anger. Allow your body to do what it needs to do.

Four rules:

- Do not hurt anyone else.

- Do not hurt yourself.

- Do not damage or destroy anything of value.

- Do this alone only if you are confident that you can control your impulses. If you are not sure, seek out one or more people you trust to act as monitors for you. Or seek professional help.

Attacking motions to express anger that can be done at home:

- Roll up a magazine or newspaper and put tape around it, then pound the kitchen counter with it.

- Punch or kick pillows.

- Throw rolls of toilet paper at the bathroom wall.

- Throw a rug over a railing and pound it with a broom.

- Tear or cut up an old bedsheet.

- Stomp on bubble packing material.

- Stomp up and down the stairs.

How to Help Others Help Themselves

When people are contained/repressed for any length of time, tension builds. In these instances, plan/suggest healthy activities to release the tension, such as pillow fights or water fights. Challenge each member of the family/group to come up with a different game/activity to release the tension (i.e., belly laughter, dancing, singing, etc.).

Key Takeaways:

- Connection is the antidote to alienation.

- The one thing you can control is the quality of your relationship with yourself.

- Anger is typically a secondary feeling.

- Create moments of hope by carving out time to forget what is going on in the world.

About the Author

Dr. Bea Mackay is a Registered Psychologist who has been helping people reclaim their lives through individual, couples, and family therapy for over 30 years. She earned her Master's degree and Ph.D. from UBC. She is also the author of the therapist training manual, *Two-You Work: How to Work with the Self in Conflict* (2011). It has been called a "monumental achievement" and a "fine contribution to counselling and psychology literature" by Ansel Woldt, Emeritus Professor, Kent State University, and the founding member of the Association for the Advancement of Gestalt Therapy. Dr. Mackay is also a senior trainer with Gestalt Vancouver, and she facilitates workshops and lectures at conferences, top universities, and training centers in Canada, the USA, Europe, and Australia. She lives in Vancouver, British Columbia, where she enjoys hiking, biking, swimming, walking, and spending time with her son and his family.

CPSIA information can be obtained
at www.ICGtesting.com
Printed in the USA
BVHW052243151221
623840BV00003B/16/J